Byways of America

Let us go back
To the simpler and better things;
Let us retrace our steps
From our greed-born bickerings
Back to the quietness
Of plain, good friendliness.

Let us go back
To the old roads of beauty's quest;
Let us again find joy
In the fields and the woods, possessed
By the thrill of the spring,
And of summer wandering.

Thomas Curtis Clark

IDEALS PUBLICATIONS INCORPORATED
NASHVILLE, TENNESSEE

Publisher, Patricia A. Pingry; Editor, Nancy J. Skarmeas; Art Director, Patrick T. McRae; Copy Editor, Laura Matter
Illustrated maps by Susan J. Harrison

Published by Ideals Publications Incorporated, 535 Metroplex Drive, Suite 250, Nashville, Tennessee 37211
Printed and bound in the U.S.A. by R.R. Donnelley & Sons.

Library of Congress Catalog Card No: 94-155410
ISBN 0-8249-4053-9

Cover: Grist Mill, Sudbury, Massachusetts, Dick Dietrich Photography

CONTENTS

*Country lanes and covered bridges,
old stone walls and the brilliant colors
of autumn . . . northern New England
offers untold treasures to the
byway traveler. From a small town
maple sugar festival welcoming
the first signs of spring to a
proud old lighthouse standing
guard on the rocky coast,
the region is a wealth of
tradition and a showcase of
classic American landscapes.*

COUNTRY LANES
AND COVERED BRIDGES

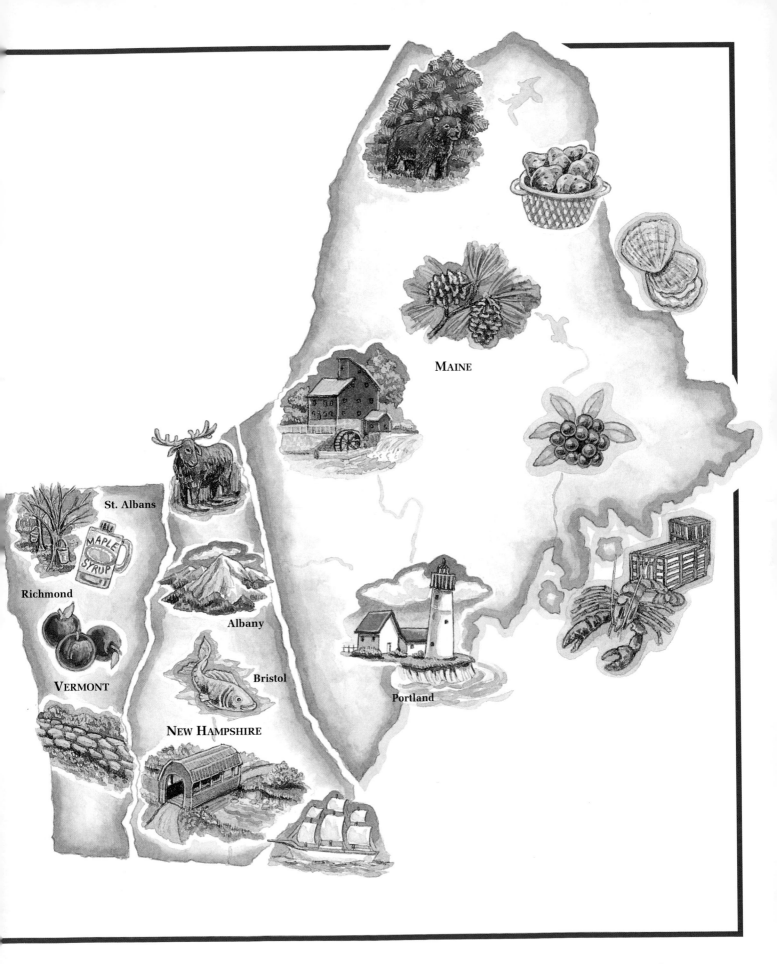

MAINE

St. Albans

Richmond

VERMONT

Albany

Bristol

NEW HAMPSHIRE

Portland

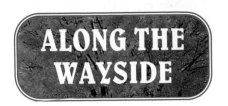

October

Robert Frost

O hushed October morning mild,
Thy leaves have ripened to the fall;
Tomorrow's wind, if it be wild,
Should waste them all.
The crows above the forest call;
Tomorrow they may form and go.
O hushed October morning mild,
Begin the hours of this day slow.
Make the day seem to us less brief.
Hearts not averse to being beguiled,
Beguile us in the way you know.
Release one leaf at break of day;
At noon release another leaf;
One from our trees, one far away.
Retard the sun with gentle mist;
Enchant the land with amethyst.
Slow, slow!
For the grapes' sake, if they were all,
Whose leaves already are burnt with frost,
Whose clustered fruit must else be lost—
For the grapes' sake along the wall.

To those in other regions of the country, it may seem that it is always autumn in New England; but local residents know to savor byway scenes, like this one along a country lane in Reading, Vermont, because the glorious golden landscape lasts only a few weeks. November ushers in the long, cold winter, which in many parts of Maine, New Hampshire, and Vermont lasts well into April.

The Bridge
Henry Wadsworth Longfellow

I stood on the bridge at midnight,
As the clocks were striking the hour,
And the moon rose o'er the city,
Behind the dark church tower.

I saw her bright reflection
In the waters under me,
Like a golden goblet falling
And sinking into the sea . . .

Whenever I cross the river
On its bridge with wooden piers,
Like the odor of brine from the ocean
Come the thoughts of other years.

And I think of how many thousands
Of care-encumbered men,
Each bearing his burden of sorrow,
Have crossed the bridge since then.

I see the long procession
Still passing to and fro,
The young heart hot and restless,
And the old subdued and slow.

And forever and forever,
As long as the river flows,
As long as the heart has passions,
And as long as life has woes,

The moon and its broken reflection
And its shadows shall appear
As the symbol of love in heaven,
And its wavering image here.

More than fifty covered bridges span the rivers of New Hampshire, some still providing safe passage after more than a century and a half. Bridges were originally covered to protect the wooden trusswork from the elements. Today, steel reinforcements have made many of the roofs unnecessary, but the bridges are faithfully preserved by New Englanders aware of the simple, priceless pleasure of coming upon a charming old covered bridge on a country drive. The Albany Bridge, pictured at left, stretches more than one hundred feet across the Swift River in Albany, New Hampshire.

The Art of Fly Tying

THE ART OF FLY TYING IS AN ancient one, going back to the twelfth century in China. Through the centuries, hand-tied fishing flies have evolved from a simple collection of horse hairs attached to a line to the present day, when the seasoned fisherman carries a fly box full of complex creations, made with everything from the discarded feathers of exotic birds to silvery man-made chenille.

Today's New England fly fishermen approach their local rivers, brooks, and ponds armed with a wide selection of flies. Confident technicians, they match their fly selection to the season, the time of day, and the life cycle of the current insect hatch. The aim is simple: to create a fly realistic enough to blend with the insect life of the river and to convince the wary trout to take the lure.

Across northern New England, fly fishing season generally runs from April to October; the months in between are spent at the fly-tying bench, working on technique and dreaming of the perfect fly, the perfect fish, and the perfect river.

The Swift River, which runs along the Kancamagus Highway in northern New Hampshire's White Mountains, is one of the countless rivers, brooks, and streams throughout the region that support trout and, thus, lure local fly fishermen. The sport demands skill, patience, and concentration; in return it promises the faithful angler a glimpse into the perfectly balanced world of fish, river, and nature.

Maple Sugaring Time

EVERY APRIL, THE RESIDENTS OF St. Albans, in far northern Vermont, gather for a celebration that is repeated throughout the late winter and early spring in towns across northern New England: the annual maple sugar festival. There is much to celebrate. Maple sugar gives a boost to the local economy, a sweetness to breakfast tables throughout the country, and a lift to sagging spirits weary of the long, cold, snowy New England winter. In St. Albans, as elsewhere, local residents gather together to taste maple delicacies, to watch the sticky sap boil down to thick, sweet maple syrup, and to declare their faith that spring will arrive, despite the snow—still often measured in feet—and the bare tree limbs against steel gray skies.

Maple sugar festivals offer the chance to taste and rate the year's crop, and they remind everyone that maple syrup is about more than pancakes: maple muffins, maple gravy, maple candy, and many more special treats featuring the sweet springtime sap are available at every festival. To byway travelers searching for a taste of northern New England, there is no better place than a small-town maple sugar festival.

Maple Muffins

Preheat oven to 350°. Lightly grease 20 muffin cups. Combine 1½ cups all-purpose flour, 1½ cups old-fashioned oats, 1 tablespoon cinnamon, 2 teaspoons baking powder, and 1 teaspoon baking soda. Set aside. Combine 2 beaten eggs, 1 cup heavy cream, and 1 cup maple syrup. Add dry mixture to egg mixture, stirring just until combined. Add 1 cup chopped dates and 1 cup walnuts, if desired. Fill muffin cups with batter. Drizzle an additional ⅓-cup maple syrup over tops. Bake 20 minutes or until a toothpick inserted into center of muffin comes out dry. Serve warm with butter. Makes 20 muffins.

Maple Cream Candy

Place 2 cups maple syrup into a saucepan and boil over very low heat without stirring until temperature reaches 233°. Pour into a shallow pan; without stirring, cool to 110° or until lukewarm. Beat until light in color and creamy in texture. Pour into a greased pan. Let cool; cover tightly to store.

Steam rises from a sugar house in Bristol, New Hampshire: a sure sign that inside raw maple sap is on its way to becoming sweet, delicious maple syrup. Locals know that a sugar house—a small wooden structure devoted solely to the purpose of boiling sap—and never a family kitchen, is the place to make syrup, for the steam is full of sticky maple that will coat everything it touches.

Evening in a Sugar Orchard

Robert Frost

From where I lingered in a lull in March
Outside a sugarhouse one night for choice,
I called the fireman with a careful voice
And bade him leave the pan and stoke the arch:
"O fireman, give the fire another stoke,
And send more sparks up the chimney with the smoke."
I thought a few might tangle, as they did,
Among bare maple boughs, and in the rare
Hill atmosphere not cease to glow,
And so be added to the moon up there.
The moon, though slight, was moon enough to show
On every tree a bucket with a lid,
And on black ground a bear-skin rug of snow.
The sparks made no attempt to be the moon.
They were content to figure in the trees
As Leo, Orion, and Pleiades.
And that was what the boughs were full of soon.

Although the bare limbs and snow cover suggest winter, the silver buckets hanging from the trunk of this giant old maple mean only one thing: spring will soon arrive in northern New England and, with it, maple sap. Even when the change in season is all but imperceptible to human senses, the maples react to the lengthening, slowly warming days and still-cold nights of late February and early March with a generous flow of sap, with more than enough to spare for the eager farmers ready to harvest their first crop of the year. This veteran tree stands outside a meeting house in Sanbornton, New Hampshire.

Maine's Portland Head Lighthouse has been guiding travelers to shore for more than two hundred years. Legislators ordered work begun on the lighthouse in the late 1780s when Portland was the nation's sixth largest port but had no lighthouse to guide ships to safety on its often treacherous rocky shore. The first light flickered at Portland Head on January 10, 1791. Since that day, Portland Head has been celebrated in the paintings of Edward Hopper and in the poetry of Henry Wadsworth Longfellow; and it has earned a place in American hearts as one of the treasures of coastal Maine.

Countless small towns in northern New England proudly feature a beautiful old, white clapboard church built at the center of town by the earliest settlers. Richmond, in northwestern Vermont, offers a slight variation on the theme, with a sixteen-sided round church. Built in 1813 as a combination house of worship and community center, the church, like most in the region, is maintained in meticulous condition by residents proud of their local heritage.

Rocky coastlines and roadside heritage define the three southernmost New England states. Nothing has shaped this area more than the great Atlantic Ocean, and nothing is prized more by the people in this region than their central role in American history. The results are evident to travelers, who find charming island villages, replete with the flavor of the sea, and restored colonial towns that preserve the story of some of the very first American settlers to cross the Atlantic.

Hancock

Deerfield

Litchfield

ROCKY COASTLINES AND ROADSIDE HERITAGE

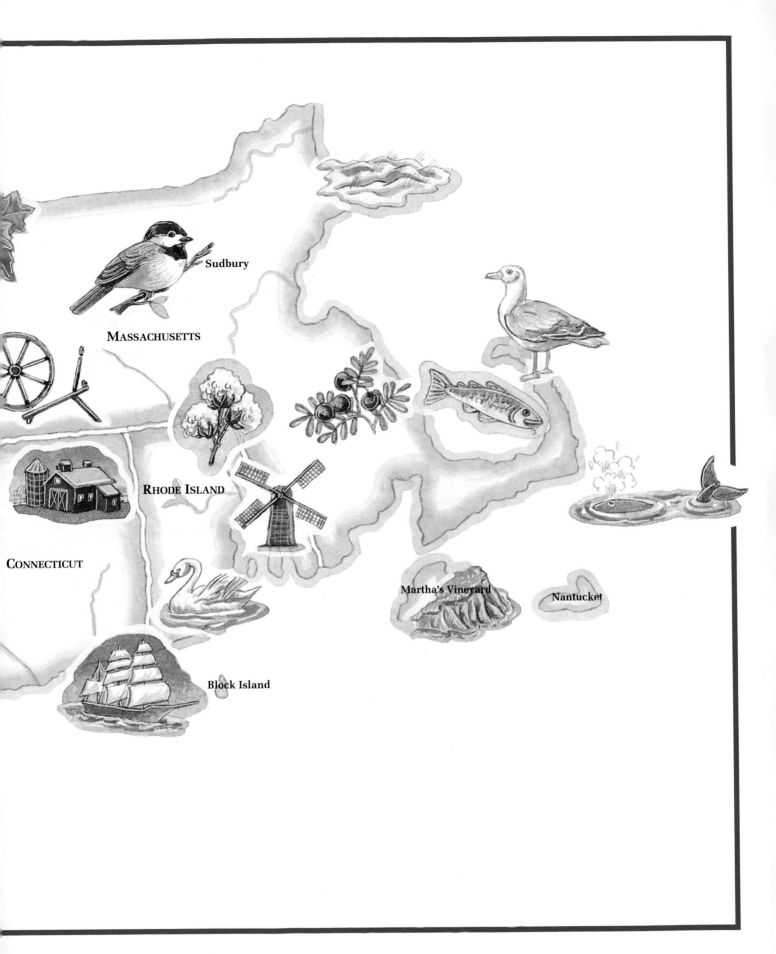

Sudbury

MASSACHUSETTS

RHODE ISLAND

CONNECTICUT

Martha's Vineyard

Nantucket

Block Island

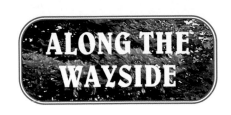
Sea Memories

Henry Wadsworth Longfellow

Often I think of the beautiful town
That is seated by the sea;
Often in thought I go up and down
The pleasant streets of that dear old town,
And my youth comes back to me.
And a verse of a Lapland song
Is haunting my memory still:
"A boy's will is the wind's will,
And the thoughts of youth are long, long thoughts."

I can see the shadowy lines of its trees
And catch, in sudden gleams,
The sheen of the far-surrounding seas,
And islands that were the Hesperides
Of all my boyish dreams.
And the burdens of that old song,
It murmurs and whispers still:
"A boy's will is the wind's will,
And the thoughts of youth are long, long thoughts."

I remember the black wharves and the ships,
And the sea-tides tossing free,
And the Spanish sailors with bearded lips,
And the beauty and mystery of the ships,
And the magic of the sea.
And the voice of that wayward song
Is singing and saying still:
"A boy's will is the wind's will,
And the thoughts of youth are long, long thoughts."

The quaint, cobblestone streets of the villages of Martha's Vineyard and Nantucket islands seem a world apart from the modern mainland, although the coast of their mother state, Massachusetts is only fifty miles away. The beautiful captains' homes and charming shingled cottages that grace both islands are remnants of the days more than one hundred and fifty years ago when the whaling industry briefly turned these sleepy islands into bustling seaports. This rose-lined picket fence runs along the streets of Edgartown, on Martha's Vineyard.

Sea Fever

John Masefield

I must go down to the seas again,
To the lonely sea and the sky;
And all I ask is a tall ship
And a star to steer her by,
And the wheel's kick, and the wind's song
And the white sail's shaking,
And a gray mist on the sea's face,
And a gray dawn breaking.

I must go down to the seas again,
For the call of the running tide
Is a wild call and a clear call
That may not be denied;
And all I ask is a windy day
With the white clouds flying,
And the flung spray and the blown spume,
And the sea gulls crying.

I must go down to the seas again,
To the vagrant gypsy life,
To the gull's way and the whale's way,
Where the wind's like a whetted knife;
And all I ask is a merry yarn
From a laughing fellow-rover,
And quiet sleep and a sweet dream
When the long trick's over.

More than anything else, it is the sea that shapes the states of southern New England. Rhode Island alone—the nation's tiniest state, measuring not quite fifty miles from north to south and slightly less from east to west—boasts an unbelievable four hundred miles of coastline. This breathtaking view of the Gay Head Cliffs on Martha's Vineyard, Massachusetts, is one of the more spectacular coastline views in the region.

Stability

Edna Jaques

The solid fundamental things of earth
That never change no matter what the age:
Buck brush and willows by a shiny pond,
A summer morning and the smell of sage;

Old-fashioned virtues, that we often see:
Clear-minded men and women fine and strong,
A young boy happy in his chosen work
Starting a summer morning with a song;

Hitching a brown team to a walking plow,
Plowing a field as if to the manner born,
Rejoicing at the sight of greening fields
And golden tassels forming on the corn;

A couple, middle-aged, yet finding still
The dear companionship of younger days,
A lantern hanging in a dingy barn
Making a golden circle with its rays;

A sturdy cottage on a village street,
A church door open to the passer-by,
A mother leading home a tired child,
A blue star glowing in the twilight sky;

These are the things of piety and worth
That hold together all of God's earth.

Any drive along the backroads of western Massachusetts and Connecticut will lead through a village like Deerfield. It is hard to think of Deerfield, located in the Pioneer Valley of central Massachusetts, as a frontier town, but in 1669, that's just what the village was—an isolated outpost of New England. Settlers came to Deerfield anxious to claim the rich farmland along the Connecticut River but found themselves more concerned with survival than farming. Today, as a tribute to the tenacity of their forefathers, the townspeople proudly maintain the village in its colonial form. Here, the restored Dwight House and its barn create a picture-perfect colonial New England scene.

Hancock Shaker Village

ONE HUNDRED AND FIFTY YEARS ago, the three hundred members of the City of Peace Shaker community gathered in Hancock, in western Massachusetts. They settled here to live a life built upon the virtues of simplicity and utility.

At the center of that way of life was farming, which the Shakers pursued with the diligence, commitment, and common sense typical of a people who believed that perfect utility creates perfect beauty. They farmed their land with studied economy, getting the most from the earth without waste or excess, and in the process made important innovations that were useful to their fellow farmers across western Massachusetts.

No Shakers remain in Hancock, but the village is faithfully maintained by a group of dedicated people who believe there is much to be learned from the Shaker approach to life. One thousand acres of village land are still devoted to farming based upon the Shaker methods. The village is open to visitors, who will find in Hancock a lesson in local history and farming, a peaceful retreat, and, more likely than not, a bit of inspiration. The Shaker Village has become part of the culture of the Berkshires, and no trip through these soft green hills would be complete without a day spent in Hancock.

The stunning Round Stone Barn at the center of Hancock Shaker Village is a tribute to the Shaker way of life. While the barn is admired today for its architectural magnificence, its value to the Shakers was functional rather than aesthetic. One farmhand, working in the center of the barn—where a central manger held hay loaded in from a balcony above—could feed a herd of cattle quickly and efficiently.

The Same Things Over

Douglas Malloch

The farmer plows the same soil over,
Plants this year's corn on last year's clover,
Walks the new rows
That this year knows,
Where last year's rows are seen no more,
And finds that some new harvest grows
Where some old harvest grew before.

And like the farmer's field is duty:
The oldest task has some new beauty.
At morning's sound
The same old ground
We plow, and walk the same old ways;
But call it not "the same old round"—
Today's task is always today's.

Who drives a spindle, writes a letter,
I know each day can do it better,
Love some task more
Than loved before,
Make some more nobly fashioned thing.
Ah, yes, we plow the same soil o'er,
But every morning it is spring.

Although farming has largely disappeared from the more populated areas of Massachusetts, Connecticut, and Rhode Island, farms like this one on Rhode Island's tiny, picturesque Block Island can still be found along the rural roads of all three states. With stone walls marking boundaries along soft green rolling hills, scenes like this one remain almost unchanged from the days of the first settlers more than three hundred and fifty years ago.

Litchfield, Connecticut, has often been called the perfect New England village. Settled in 1720 as a frontier outpost, Litchfield became a center of colonial activity during the Revolutionary War. In perhaps the village's most famous act of patriotism, the women of Litchfield melted a statue of King George III of England and turned the metal into bullets for the colonial army. The village was the birthplace of such American notables as Ethan Allen, Henry Ward Beecher, and Harriet Beecher Stowe. It was also the location of the first American law school, an institution that graduated two vice-presidents, three Supreme Court justices, and one hundred and twenty congressmen. But life changed dramatically in Litchfield when the railroad came to western Connecticut, bypassing the village and leaving it off the fast track of nineteenth-century American life. As a result, much in Litchfield remains unchanged from the years just after the American Revolution. Stately colonial houses surround the village green, a white church steeple rises against the sky, and the atmosphere is perfect for a quiet stroll through another era.

This beautiful stone grist mill sits on the grounds of The Wayside Inn in Sudbury, Massachusetts. The inn, also known as The Red Horse Inn, was immortalized in Henry Wadsworth Longfellow's poem "Tales of a Wayside Inn," which follows the form of Chaucer's "The Canterbury Tales," telling the stories of a group of travelers stopping for the night at the Red Horse Inn. For more than two hundred and fifty years, the inn has offered "food, drink, and lodging for man or beast," and the picturesque mill, although no longer a functioning grist mill, still provides inspiration for artists and photographers, as well as a peaceful rest stop for travelers along the old Boston Post Road in eastern Massachusetts.

PASTORAL TREASURES ALONG COUNTRY ROADS
await byway travelers who leave
behind the big cities of New York,
New Jersey, and Pennsylvania
to seek out quieter pleasures.
A Pennsylvania Dutch folk festival will
fill a summer weekend with local food,
crafts, and music; an autumn hike through
the Adirondack wilderness of upstate
New York will reveal colors unmatched
on the planet; and exploration of endless
backroads will prove that although these
states may be known more for their
cities, they boast some of the most
enchanting countryside in America.

PASTORAL TREASURES
─ALONG COUNTRY ROADS─

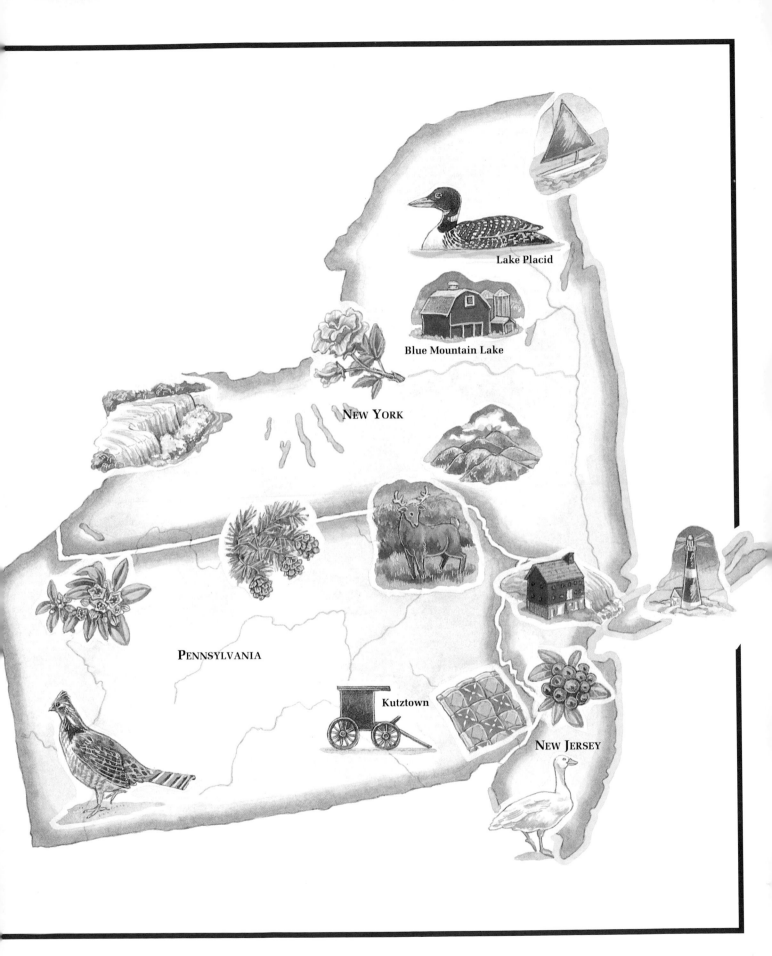

Lake Placid

Blue Mountain Lake

NEW YORK

PENNSYLVANIA

Kutztown

NEW JERSEY

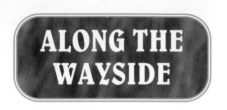

Summer

Hal Borland

I never remember in April how tall the grass will be
in the pastures and hay fields in June. Or that daisies will
frost the fence row and buttercups gild the meadow.
I forget that the choke cherries will be in bloom with
their sharp-tanged fragrance, and that June is other
things than roses and honeysuckle.

June is really a time of relative quiet, serenity after the
rush of sprouting and leafing and flowering and before the
fierce heat that drives toward maturity and seed. June's
air can be as sweet as the wild strawberries that will
grace its middle weeks, sweet as clover, a sweetness that
might be cloying if it weren't still so new.

Birds are singing at their best, not only morning and evening
but all through the day. The oriole, the tanager, and the robin
can make an early day vibrate with song, and a part of the
song seemed this morning to be in the air even when I couldn't
hear a bird note. The rasping that is July and August, the
scraping of cicada and all their kin, is yet in abeyance.
June doesn't assault the ears. It flatters them and softens the
call of the frog and the whippoorwill and is a joy.

These things I seem to have to learn all over again each
June, and I wonder how I could have forgotten. I shall forget
them again, and next March I shall think of June and roses
and wonder what else it was that made last June so
wonderful. Then June will come again and I shall find it a
happy memory rediscovered and ready to live again.

For almost four hundred years, farmers have worked the fertile soil of southeastern Pennsylvania's Lancaster County. The first to come were William Penn and his Quaker brethren, but the colony's reputation for religious tolerance as well as fertile farmlands drew Amish, Mennonites, and others, known collectively now as the Pennsylvania Dutch. These hard-working people provided food for colonial America and turned the soft hills of southeastern Pennsylvania into a patchwork of fields that remains one of the most beautiful landscapes in the eastern United States, drawing visitors from across the country eager to immerse themselves in the peaceful life of the Pennsylvania Dutch. This farmhouse sits nestled behind a field of wheat in the heart of Lancaster County.

The Covered Bridge

Erma Stull Grove

One comes upon it suddenly,
Around a curve and down a hill,
And there it is: the covered bridge,
Centuries old, but useful still.

There's a tingle that goes up the spine
As one enters the shadowed place,
For in that instant one is sure
It bridges time as well as space.

Built for the horse-and-buggy days
The bridge has seen changes galore:
Few horses cross the span these days,
Just automobiles by the score.

Gone is the leisure to saunter,
To hunt berries or pick wildflowers,
To skip pebbles across the stream
And watch the ripples for hours.

Too often today one hurries,
Always rushing to get somewhere,
But this bridge seems to say, "Slow down,
Take your time from worries and care."

As you rattle across the planks
Or peer through the cracks on the side,
Recall some memories from the past,
And take on your future in stride.

Driving the backroads of Lancaster County, Pennsylvania, one is likely to come across more than a few old covered bridges, and just as likely to see them crossed by an Amish buggy as by a modern automobile. A buggy with a gray top belongs to an Amish family, while the all-black buggies carry Old Order Mennonites.

The Kutztown Folk Festival

FOR TEN DAYS EACH SUMMER, IN the charming southeastern Pennsylvania town of Kutztown, families gather together for the traditional Pennsylvania Dutch Folk Festival. The festival features Pennsylvania Dutch crafts, like glass blowing and knitting; a country kitchen where old Pennsylvania Dutch specialties are prepared on an old-fashioned wood-burning cookstove; sheep shearing and horseshoeing done the old-fashioned way; and, perhaps most anticipated of all, the annual quilting contest, which displays and sells the best work of local quilters.

The festival is a joyous event, with traditional music and folk dancing performances every day. There are also opportunities to learn about the life and customs of the Pennsylvania Dutch in seminars and workshops ranging from hands-on instruction in "The Skills of Woodworking" to talks by experts on such things as Pennsylvania Dutch costumes and herb gardening.

The annual Kutztown Folk Festival preserves the wonderful heritage of the Pennsylvania Dutch, a small group of Americans whose unique way of life has touched us all. Those travelers who are looking for a true slice of good old-fashioned Americana need look no further than Kutztown each July.

Quilting is a large part of the life of many Pennsylvania Dutch women. Mothers, daughters, and granddaughters gather together to make quilts to give to family and friends, and also to sell to the tourists who come through their towns in search of their beautiful handiwork. Because they have remained such a cohesive community since coming to America, the various groups of Pennsylvania Dutch have held on to the quilting traditions of their German ancestors. Features that identify a Pennsylvania Dutch quilt include bright, contrasting colors, exquisite needlework, and traditional German symbols, such as the heart in a wreath, which signifies the blessing of a home, and the double rose or tulip set in three lobes, which represents the Trinity.

The Adirondack Museum

IN THE HEART OF THE ALMOST ten thousand square miles of wilderness in upstate New York's Adirondack Park, byway travelers will discover a wonderful treasure — the Adirondack Museum. Nestled between sparkling blue lakes and beautiful mountain slopes, the museum is dedicated to preserving the heritage of northern New York's mountain region, the beauty of which has attracted adventurers and vacationers for two centuries.

Why people have journeyed to the Adirondacks is obvious to anyone who has seen the breathtaking, pristine landscape. The museum documents the first tourists of the early nineteenth century who took the twenty-six-hour trip from New York City in search of fresh air. Rustic cabins deep in the woods housed intrepid adventurers, whereas more refined visitors preferred the lovely resorts that flourished in the 1880s.

Whatever their personal style, however, travelers then, as travelers now, could not have been disappointed by the natural beauty of the Adirondacks; and inside the rustic buildings of the Adirondack Museum, today's adventurers can trace their connection to those who came before them.

Sunflowers bloom profusely against the backdrop of the Adirondack Mountains near Lake Placid, New York. Most of the mountain range is contained within Adirondack State Park, which the state of New York has pledged to keep "forever wild." The first known tourists to travel through the Adirondacks were a group of Yale students who made the trip in 1818. Since then, the mountains and their accompanying series of rivers and lakes have been treasured by Easterners as an accessible escape from their crowded cities.

Farm in Heaven

Nancy Byrd Turner

When years went by like some bright charm
And mine had numbered seven,
We spent one summer on a farm
That must have been in heaven.

The very lanes were paved with gold,
And on the high bright hills
Were jewels more than hands could hold,
All cut like daffodils.

A stream went running clear and wide
Through pasture lands and dales;
The creatures in its crystal tide
Had tails like minnow-tails.

The garden gate was carved from pearl;
I swung upon it wild—
An angel and a little girl,
A cherub and a child.

At dusk and dawn fell honey-dew
And manna, all around;
Whichever way the four winds blew
A harp began to sound.

And by what road I came away
My heart forgets, but when
Life gives me time to try, some day,
I'll find that trail again!

Although winters average one hundred inches of snow and the normal growing season is only three months long, many of the permanent residents of the Adirondacks still make their living by farming. Scenes like this one—a stately red barn set against the early fall mountainside—are evidence that while life may be a challenge in northern New York, the rewards for meeting that challenge are magnificent.

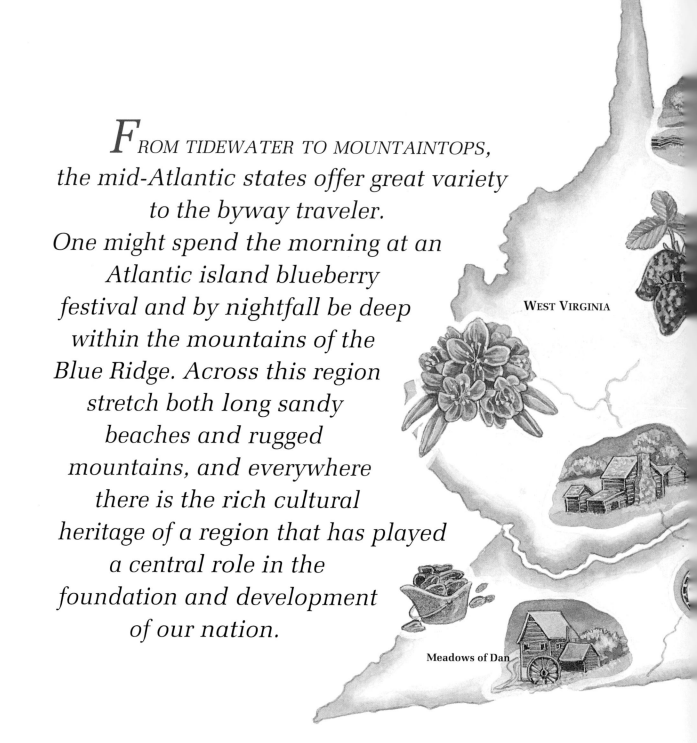

FROM TIDEWATER TO MOUNTAINTOPS,
the mid-Atlantic states offer great variety
to the byway traveler.
One might spend the morning at an
Atlantic island blueberry
festival and by nightfall be deep
within the mountains of the
Blue Ridge. Across this region
stretch both long sandy
beaches and rugged
mountains, and everywhere
there is the rich cultural
heritage of a region that has played
a central role in the
foundation and development
of our nation.

WEST VIRGINIA

Meadows of Dan

FROM TIDEWATER
TO MOUNTAINTOPS

MARYLAND

DELAWARE

VIRGINIA

Chincoteague Island

Ferrum

Wayside Temptation

Agnes Finch Whitacre

We took the winding road
Across the countryside,
Over hill and dale,
Along a river wide.

We found a shady glen
Snug in a lovely cove,
With daisies all in bloom,
As on and on we drove.

The trees wore springtime green;
The fields were waving grain;
All was peace and quiet,
Away from city strain.

I longed to stop beside
A rippling little stream
Along the wooded wayside
To lie awhile and dream.

Tempting wildflower meadows like this one abound along Virginia's Blue Ridge Parkway, a winding road through the spectacular Blue Ridge Mountains. Over four hundred miles of road combine breathtaking mountain scenery with pioneer heritage, offering countless opportunities to pull off the side of the road and explore. Travelers along the Blue Ridge Parkway might be rewarded with the sight of a foraging black bear, or the discovery of a tiny craft shop selling the work of a local artisan, or the simple pleasure of a peaceful hike through spectacular autumn woods.

Wagons
Glenn Ward Dresbach

An empty wagon makes the loudest sound—
But I have heard filled wagons turn to song
Down lanes where glory lingered on the ground
Until it seemed a pageant marched along.
From old roads, hidden by the wood or hill,
Drifts back the heartening rhythm wagons know
When field or wood the sturdy boxes fill
And wheels turn home, deliberate and slow.

At lonely bridges far-off thunder wakes
Like memories responding to the wheels . . .
And more each year, when wind grows
cold and shakes
The leaves before it, something in me feels
The need to hear, above the rattling husk,
The sound of loaded wagons in the dusk.

The Blue Ridge Mountains were one of the first American frontiers, leading settlers southward to the Appalachians of North Carolina and Tennessee. Evidence of these pioneer days can be found all along the Blue Ridge Parkway, where abandoned woodland cabins and wagons like this one speak of a way of life long since disappeared.

Chincoteague Island Blueberry Festival and Craft Show

JULY IS A BEAUTIFUL MONTH ON tiny Chincoteague Island, which is cradled in the ocean just off the coast of Virginia. The temperatures are warm, as on the mainland, but cool Atlantic sea breezes soften the air, creating the perfect atmosphere for the annual Blueberry Festival and Craft Show.

The blueberry is the star of the day, with plump local specimens for sale alone or as part of wonderful pies, muffins, ice creams, and more. The festival, which benefits a local hospital fund, is truly a family day. There are plenty of games for the children and live entertainment throughout the afternoon. And when visitors have eaten their fill of tasty Virginia blueberries, there are countless craft booths to explore, featuring the work of local artisans, from the patient sculptors who carve the famous Chincoteague duck decoys to the painters who find inspiration on the island's pristine beaches for their beautiful watercolors.

Finish the day with a leisurely walk around the island, a true gem for the summer traveler with a love of the ocean.

Fresh Blueberry Jam

Fresh-picked blueberries make the most wonderful jam, preserving the flavor of July all through the year. This recipe can be adapted for any amount of blueberries; simply use 1 cup of sugar for each cup of fresh berries.

Wash and measure blueberries. Place them in a heavy stainless steel pan and crush the bottom layer. Cook over moderate heat, adding a half cup of water. Simmer until the blueberries are almost tender. Add sugar (1 cup for each cup of berries). Cook and stir over low heat until the jam consistency is reached. (Test by dropping a small spoonful on a plate. If it holds its shape, the jam is ready.) Pour jam into hot, sterilized jars.

The wild pony is a nationally recognized symbol of Chincoteague Island. The ponies are descendants of domestic stock left on the island by seventeenth-century settlers. These wild ponies, along with the thousands of migrating shorebirds who make a temporary home in Chincoteague National Wildlife Refuge, share the island with human inhabitants, whose charming island villages are a treasure for travelers seeking to get away from the rush of the mainland.

Blue Ridge Draft Horse and Mule Show

SHIRES, BELGIANS, SUFFOLKS, Percherons, Clydesdales—the gentle giants of the horse world—are the main attraction at the annual Draft Horse and Mule Show at Ferrum College's Blue Ridge Farm Museum in southwestern Virginia. The museum is dedicated to preserving the heritage of the nineteenth-century German-Americans who settled this part of the Blue Ridge, and the horse and mule show is a tribute to the massive animals who made the hard work of clearing the land and growing crops possible.

The horses come from all over the eastern United States to compete in a series of events based on their working history. There are pulling and plowing contests as well as obstacle driving contests in which the horses pull carts or wagons around a set course.

The pulling contests begin with a weight of two thousand pounds, which the teams of horses must pull over fifteen feet. The animals need no prodding to go to work. At the sound of the metal hook dropping into the eye of the sled, they are off, driving their massive limbs forward. The weight increases until all but one team is eliminated, and every last spectator is thoroughly impressed.

A sight unfamiliar to most in the audience is the coon mule jumping competition. This is a remnant of the days when hunters rode their mules behind the hounds on nighttime racoon hunts. When they came to a fence—which the racoon and dogs could easily slip under—the mules would stop, wait for the hunter to throw his coat over the fence to mark its height, and then leap the fence from a standing start, ready to continue the chase on the opposite side.

Today, draft horses have all but disappeared from American farms, replaced by gasoline powered trucks and tractors. Most of us are lucky to see a single pair at a parade or a local fair. At the Blue Ridge Farm Museum each July, however, the full day is given over to these remarkable animals: the strong, gentle, and tireless partners of our early American farmers.

Draft horses participate in wagon pulling at the annual Draft Horse and Mule Show at the Blue Ridge Farm Museum, which is a part of the Blue Ridge Institute at Ferrum College in Ferrum, Virginia. The mission of the Blue Ridge Institute is to document the rich heritage of the region and to share it with the public through events like the draft horse show. In addition to the Farm Museum, the institute also supports the Blue Ridge Heritage Archive, which collects and preserves authentic photographs, recordings, and publications important to Virginia history.

A beautiful Belgian is inspected by a judge during the halter class at the draft horse and mule show. The show is just one of many yearly events at Ferrum College that celebrate Blue Ridge culture. Perhaps the biggest of all is the annual Folklife Festival, a celebration of the crafts, foods, and music of the Virginia Blue Ridge. The festival features crafts from quilting to basket weaving, and music from simple banjo picking to gospel choirs, all with one thing in common: they are part of the unique heritage of the people of the Blue Ridge Mountains.

One of the most photographed sights along Virginia's Blue Ridge Parkway is Mabry Mill, found in the state's southwestern Blue Ridge Highlands in a town called Meadows of Dan. The historic old wooden mill offers a peaceful stopping point for travelers, as well as historical exhibits that tell the story of the area's early settlers.

Step off one of West Virginia's country roads, and you will travel back in time to the days when America was mostly farmland and the Appalachian Mountain range marked the western frontier. West Virginia is the most mountainous state east of the Mississippi, and tucked away in its many valleys, behind endless ridges, are tiny villages almost untouched by the years. Settlers first came to West Virginia in the beginning of the eighteenth century, when this mountainous region was still part of the great colony of Virginia. The settlers worked hard to clear the thick forests and make pastures and cropland on the hillsides. The trials these settlers faced forced them to band together. This, along with their isolation from the Virginia on the other side of the Blue Ridge, led them to develop a unique identity. At the start of the Civil War, West Virginia broke away from Virginia to become an independent state.

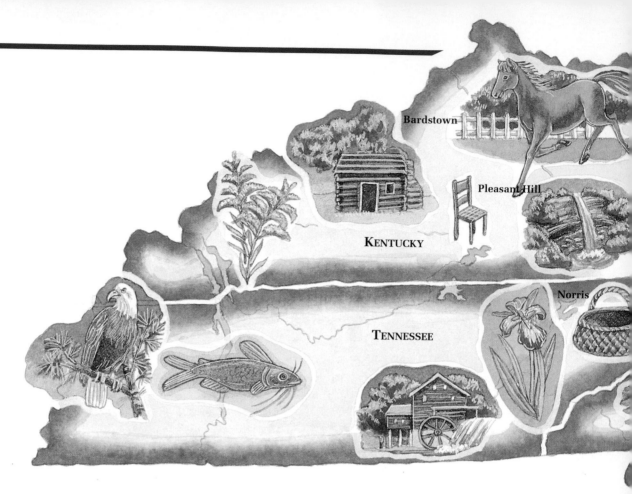

Bardstown

Pleasant Hill

KENTUCKY

TENNESSEE

Norris

*A*LONG PIONEER TRACES
and old mountain roads, travelers
to the mountains and hills of the
South will find an irresistible mix of
culture and history. In the Smoky
Mountains, Appalachian craftspeople
practice the skills passed down
to them by their grandparents;
and in the bluegrass region, a restored
village keeps alive the unique values and

ALONG
PIONEER TRACES

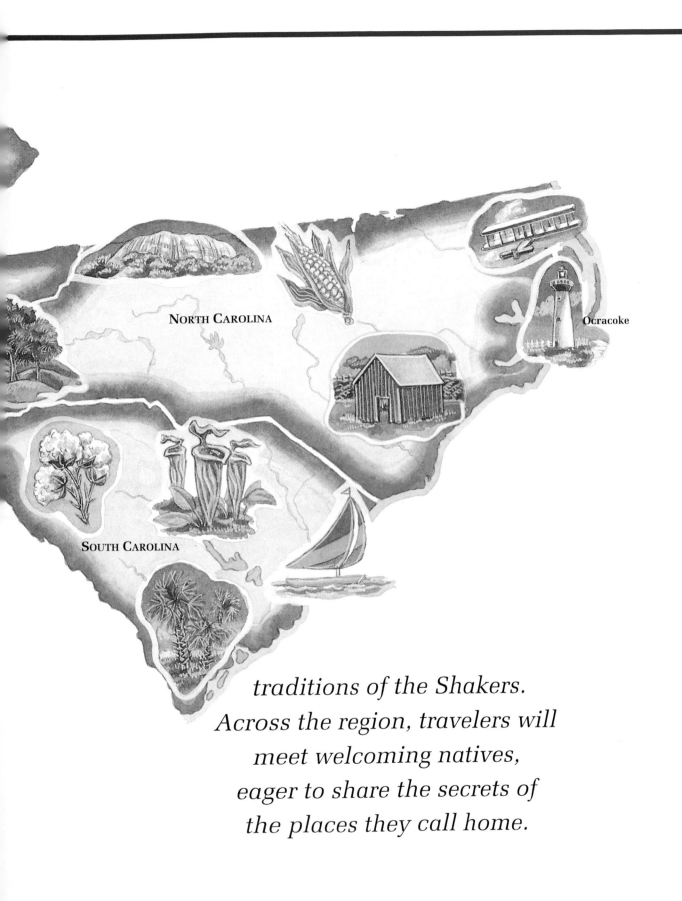

NORTH CAROLINA

Ocracoke

SOUTH CAROLINA

traditions of the Shakers.
Across the region, travelers will
meet welcoming natives,
eager to share the secrets of
the places they call home.

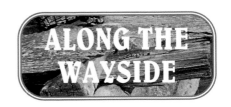

The Rail Fence
Joy Belle Burgess

This old fence long has stood
Where golden fields meet deep woods,
Where meadows boast of tender grass,
Where a babbling brook ripples past,

Undaunted by the growth of reeds
And prickly brambles that twine and cleave,
Shaggy with briars; and yet, it stands,
This rail fence, built by pioneer hands.

Guardian to all that it holds dear:
The cows rubbing their necks as they pass near,
The calves that frisk without a care,
The colts who gambol beside the mares.

A shelter for many gentle things:
The young fledgling with faltering wings,
The poised pheasant midst the weeds,
And a rabbit, listening to each rustling reed.

This old fence, rustic and grand,
Still hems the farm and the rolling land;
Where green pasture meets with rocky hill,
Where voices of the past are present still.

The history and culture of Appalachia are preserved and celebrated throughout the region, from North Carolina westward through Tennessee and Kentucky. Cades Cove, a broad, fertile valley inside Great Smoky Mountain National Park, recreates the life of the Appalachian pioneers who set deep roots in these mountains in the 1700s. Nearby Norris, Tennessee, is home to the Museum of Appalachia, which features relics from the pioneer era.

An Old Mill
Glenn Ward Dresbach

The road to its sagging doors
Is tangled in wild grape vines,
But through the sycamores,
The brook beside it shines.
Old timbers, mellowed long,
Stand firm below the hill—
And all is silent now
That the wheel
Of the mill is still.

Artists, in autumn, pause
To sketch the old mill caught
In soft lights, and because
Of something others brought
To it, we take away
Some richness from its bins—
For where dreams were once,
On another day
A dream begins.

Where some need ends, at last
Another happens by—
This old mill, holding fast
Its place against the sky,
Grinds, with no turn of wheel,
The hard shell from the kernel
Of thoughts—until
The grists reveal
Something else, eternal.

The Appalachian Mountains marked the western boundary of the American frontier until the late eighteenth century when Daniel Boone made his way through the Cumberland Gap and opened up the beautiful, fertile lands of Kentucky to settlers from the East. This rustic old mill is located on a quiet road near Bardstown, Kentucky, one of the early pioneer settlements in the state.

The Centre Family Dwelling was a place of honor in Shaker society. The Shakers believed in communal living—males and females lived as brothers and sisters, not as husband and wife. Members shared dwellings based upon their spiritual strength. The Centre Family Dwelling, closest to the community house of worship, was reserved for those community members thought to be closest to spiritual perfection. Today, the Centre Family Dwelling houses the Shaker Life and Customs exhibit which begins visitors' tours of the village.

Shakertown at Pleasant Hill

IN THE MIDDLE OF KENTUCKY'S beautiful Bluegrass region lies the little village of Pleasant Hill, a recreated Shaker community. For most of the nineteenth century, Pleasant Hill was a thriving Shaker village, with close to five hundred members. The Shakers devoted themselves to a farm that spread over three thousand acres and to their workshops, where they practiced the crafts that made everyday life possible.

Pleasant Hill today is still a functioning village, run not by Shakers but by those dedicated to the Shaker heritage. The village maintains itself not through large charitable contributions but through the work of devoted craftspeople who follow the Shaker credo that "every task completed to the best of one's ability is like a prayer to God." Workers faithfully reproduce Shaker cabinets, cedar pails, brooms, barrels, churns, and woolen goods.

The village at Pleasant Hill consists of thirty nineteenth-century buildings, with some twenty miles of original stone fencing marking pastures and boundaries. The last Shakers left Pleasant Hill in 1910, but their legacy lives on in the devoted community that keeps their simple way of life alive and preserves a piece of American history. This legacy is available for travelers visiting Shakertown as they make their way through Kentucky.

The Old Spinning Wheel

Lydia O. Jackson

A household implement of long ago,
It still, in spite of marked neglect, exudes
An heirloom loveliness of beauty-glow
That came from many quiet interludes
When nimble fingers—always at great speed—
Spun carded wool, drew out the lengthening strands
Of fluff-soft yarn that served the household's needs
And satisfied its year-round demands.

And still it is the heart wheel of the home
And occupies the cherished fireside niche,
Although it has no modern trim, no chrome,
And will not ever life's estate enrich.
But still it stands, a link with yesterday
When hardy pioneers came west and stayed.

Shaker women spun and dyed their own yarn, which they later knit and wove into clothing and blankets for the community. The Shakers were industrious workers and also innovative. American Shakers are responsible for the clothespin, the flat broom, the earliest washing machines, and one of the most popular furniture styles in the country today.

The Crafts of Appalachia

A Kentucky man practices the age-old craft of basket making.

THE TRADITIONAL CRAFTS OF THE Appalachian region have one thing in common: they began not as art for art's sake, but as practical skills, necessitated by the isolation and hardship faced by settlers in the region. Quilts made use of every valuable piece of fabric or discarded clothing and provided warmth through the cold mountain winters. Baskets and buckets carried water, stored grain, and brought vegetables in from the garden. Dulcimers, banjoes, and fiddles played the music that celebrated holidays and wed-

Handcrafted wooden dulcimers hang in a shop in Pigeon Forge, Tennessee.

dings and provided entertainment on long, dark nights. These were all essential elements of pioneer life; and since the long journey across ocean and mountains and dense woodlands hadn't allowed for much to be carried in to their new homes, the people of Appalachia learned to make what they needed.

Today, the skills that made pioneer life possible in Appalachia are celebrated through folk art that is preserved and cherished as valuable connections with local

Handmade baskets are just one of the many crafts practiced by the people of the Appalachians.

history. Devoted artisans practice the crafts of their forefathers—some continuing a tradition passed from grandmother to granddaughter, and others self-taught, out of their love and respect for Appalachian heritage. Quilts today are made to keep beds warm at night, certainly, but also to keep the patterns and skills of Appalachian quilting alive and strong. And banjoes and dulcimers are carefully crafted out of love for the traditional music that is often drowned out by more modern sounds.

Quilting is a classic American craft, carried out with great skill throughout the Appalachians.

For travelers, the tradition of craftsmanship in the region is a treasure chest waiting to be unlocked. All it takes is the patience to travel quiet country roads, where a rustic roadside sign in front of a modest country home might lead to a room full of heirloom quilts, or an old barn packed to the rafters with antiques might reveal a beautiful old dulcimer, just waiting for the caring hands that will dust it off and bring it to life once more.

An early morning drive through Kentucky's Bluegrass region promises peaceful sights like this one: thoroughbred horses grazing on the dew-soaked grass behind endless stretches of winding fences. Today, the Bluegrass region is known worldwide for its horses, perhaps the best racing stock in the world; but to settlers coming through the Cumberland Gap at the turn of the nineteenth century, the blue-hued meadows of north-central Kentucky held promise as fertile crop land. That promise was quickly fulfilled, as the limestone rich soil that gives the grass its unique blue cast also provided some of the best farmland in the country. This farm in Goshen, Kentucky, is not far from Lexington, which in the days of those prosperous early settlers became known as the "Athens of the West."

The picturesque village of Ocracoke lies on North Carolina's Outer Banks, at the southern end of the seventy-mile stretch designated as Cape Hatteras National Seashore. Its lighthouse, built in 1823, is the oldest still operating in the state. Today Ocracoke Lighthouse presides over a sleepy island village, but life on the Outer Banks has not always been so peaceful. Not only was this once the most treacherous landing point on the eastern seaboard, but Ocracoke Island was once home to a sailor named Edward Teach, also known as the pirate Blackbeard. The British captured Blackbeard in the first part of the nineteenth century, but legend has it that much of his plunder remains buried off the coast of Ocracoke Island.

Belzoni

Natchez

MISSISSIPPI

LOUISIANA

Dusty roads and Spanish moss welcome the traveler to the Deep South, lending an unmistakable flavor to the region. Full of tradition and small town charms—from the annual sorghum festival in a mountain village to the folk art of a Mississippi Delta grandmother—

DUSTY ROADS
AND SPANISH MOSS

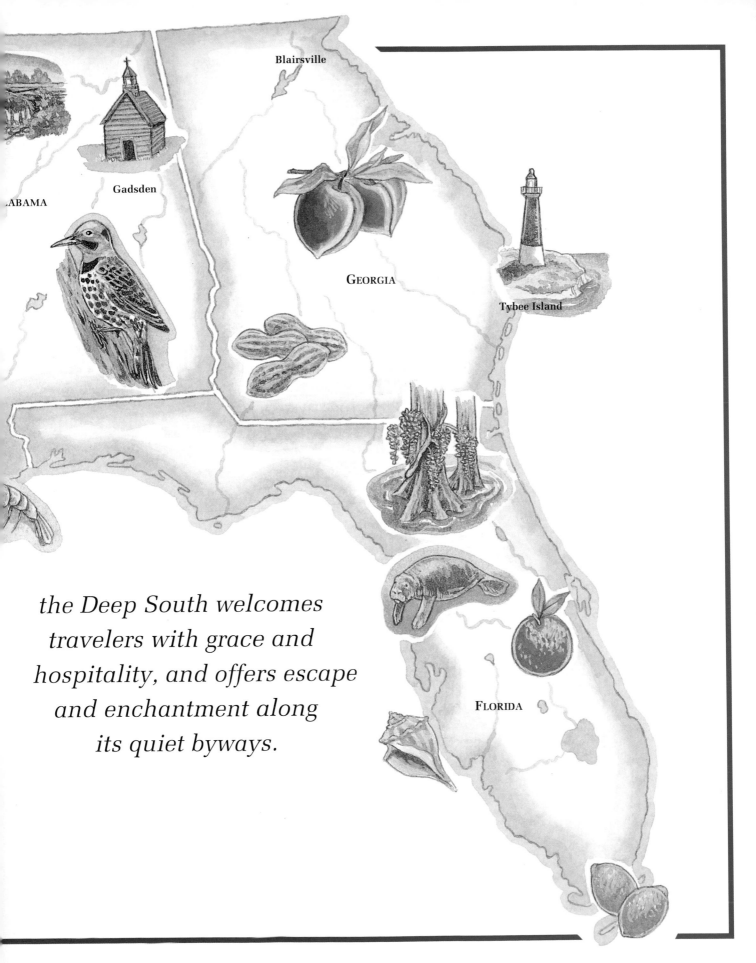

the Deep South welcomes travelers with grace and hospitality, and offers escape and enchantment along its quiet byways.

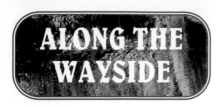

I Saw in Louisiana
a Live Oak Growing
Walt Whitman

I saw in Louisiana a live oak growing.
All alone stood it, and the moss hung down from the branches;
Without any companion it grew there uttering joyous
leaves of dark green,
And its look, rude, unbending, lusty, made me think of myself.
But I wondered how it could utter joyous leaves standing
Alone there without its friends near, for I knew I could not,
And I broke off a twig with a certain number of leaves upon it,
and twined around it a little moss,
And brought it away, and I have placed it in sight in my room.
It is not needed to remind me as of my own dear friends
(For I believe lately I think of little else than them),
Yet it remains to me a curious token; it makes me
think of manly love.
For all that, and though the live oak glistens there in
Louisiana solitary in a wide flat space,
Uttering joyous leaves all its life without a friend
or lover near,
I know very well I could not.

Spanish moss is an epiphytic plant, which means that it depends upon another plant for support but not for nutrients. Its most frequent companion is the live oak, an ever-green variety of the oak family found in the southeastern United States. After only a few years' growth, the moss begins to hang delicately from the oak limbs, creating a graceful canopy for quiet country lanes, enticing travelers with the romance of the Deep South.

O Magnet-South

Walt Whitman

O magnet-South! O glistening perfumed South! my South!
O quick mettle, rich blood, impulse and love!
Good and evil! O all dear to me!
O dear to me my birth-pangs—all moving things
and the trees where I was born—the grains, plants, rivers,
Dear to me my own slow sluggish rivers where they flow,
distant, over flats of silvery sands or through swamps,
Dear to me the Roanoke, the Savannah, the Altamahaw,
the Pedee, the Tombigbee, the Santee, the Coosa and the Sabine,
O pensive, far away wandering, I return with my soul
to haunt their banks again.
Again in Florida I float on transparent lakes, I float
on the Okeechobee, I cross the hummock-land or through
pleasant openings or dense forests;
I see the parrots in the woods, I see the papaw-tree and the blossoming titi;
Again, sailing on my coaster deck, I coast off Georgia,
I coast up the Carolinas; I see where the live-oak is growing,
I see where the yellow-pine, the scented bay-tree, the lemon and orange,
the cyprus, the graceful palmetto;
I pass rude sea-headlands and enter Pimlico sound
through an inlet, and dart my vision inland.

*The long lanes leading up to the great plantations of the Old
South were often lined with borders of azaleas, which burst
into a colorful display each spring. Today, although most of
the plantations exist only as historic sites, the azaleas remain,
and they have become one of the signature flowers of the
South, celebrated in countless festivals throughout the region.*

Natchez Trace Parkway

THOUSANDS OF YEARS AGO, Native Americans traveled across what is now the state of Mississippi following a series of footpaths leading from the Mississippi River toward the northeast, where they hunted buffalo. Their paths were the only route through the dense forests that covered the area.

As European settlers began to move into the area, they too made use of the footpaths. Meriwether Lewis, of the great exploration team of Lewis and Clark, traveled on the paths, which became known as "The Trace." So did Andrew Jackson, John J. Audubon, and the great Native American leader Tecumseh. As the area developed, the Trace also became an important route for Kentucky boatmen, who floated their cargo down the Mississippi and walked back home by way of the Trace, which took them as far north as Nashville.

In 1806, recognizing the importance of the route, the United States Congress voted to spend government money to improve the road. A year later those plans were scrapped, as the invention of the steamboat made both southward and northward travel on the Mississippi possible. The well-worn Trace became all but obsolete.

Today, a modern touring road closely follows the route of the Trace. The Natchez Trace Parkway leads travelers from the fascinating mounds left behind by the earliest native inhabitants of the Natchez area, through lush green forests, past open fields where wild turkey often mingle with white-tailed deer, northeast to Tupelo, where a museum celebrates the history of the Natchez Trace. The Parkway winds through places like French Camp and Pigeon Roost, which began as overnight camps offering food and rest for travelers. Historic markers abound along the route, helping today's traveler find his way along this wonderful route that peacefully crosses this area and faithfully preserves its rich heritage.

Barytown Tavern in Natchez, Mississippi, is reminiscent of another era, when travelers making their way along the difficult and often treacherous Natchez Trace pressed to get to the next inn before nightfall. At these inns one could feed and water the horses, sit down to a hearty meal, and enjoy a good night's sleep before the next day's journey. Today, the Trace is a modern highway, but many of the inns remain, giving a wonderful, old-fashioned flavor to the route.

The Old Sorghum Mill

Grace C. Sherrill

Built on the slope of a little hill,
Memory pictures the sorghum mill.
Farm neighbors brought cane from far and near
To make molasses in autumn each year.

Old Jack went round and round the sweep
On that never ending road he'd keep;
And stalks of cane—each time Jack passed—
Were fed to the crusher's hungry grasp.

The juice ran down into pans below
Above a furnace—a double row.
It steamed and bubbled and foamed and boiled,
While men beside it with skimmers toiled.

And when we children came to the mill,
From clean pine paddles we licked our fill
Of molasses from that long tin trough
Where it had cooled as the foam drained off.

Thoughts of the mill to my mind recall
Molasses taffy and popcorn balls,
Delicious cookies and gingerbread,
And molasses on our pancakes spread.

Smoke from the fires has faded away,
And the sweet taste of syrup belongs to that day
When the mill on the hillside turned cane to molasses
And a child knew nothing about how time passes.

Each October, in Blairsville, located in the mountains of Georgia's Union County, residents and friends gather to celebrate their favorite crop, sorghum, which is ground, crushed, and cooked into a wonderful sweet syrup. The center of the celebration is the old mill, where grinding is done both the old-fashioned way, with horses slowly turning wooden roller mills, and the modern way, with electric power replacing horse power. Either way, the result is the same wonderful sticky-sweet syrup, best served on hot homemade biscuits. Highlights of the festival are the Biscuit and Syrup Sopping Contest, a square dance, and the annual prize for the oldest participant. The Blairsville mill is one of only ten remaining in the area that carry on the tradition of sorghum making, and in so doing preserve a wonderful piece of southern mountain culture.

Mama's Dream World: Mississippi Delta Stitchery

IN THE SMALL, QUIET TOWN OF Belzoni, in west-central Mississippi, a piece of Mississippi Delta heritage is preserved in the work of craftswoman Ethel Wright Mohamed. Mohamed, known in and around Belzoni simply as the "Grandma Moses of Stitchery," created original hand-stitched "memory pictures," preserving with cloth and colored thread the experiences of her family and their neighbors in the Delta.

Although Mrs. Mohamed learned embroidery as a child, she did not pick up her needle for any other than practical reasons until her eight children were grown and her husband had passed away. Eager to keep the memories of her past alive

for her many grandchildren, Mrs. Mohamed began stitching. Each carefully stitched picture tells a story from the life of her family and community. Mrs. Mohamed's work is full of the love she felt for her family and rich with the traditions of her small Mississippi town.

Following patterns traced by hand onto grocery bags and the back side of shopping lists, Mrs. Mohamed followed no rules of precision or form in her pictures: she claimed never to have reworked a single stitch, and her color palette followed her own fancy more than the dictates of nature. Yet the results are splendid: one hundred and twenty-five pictures recreating the saga of one family, and preserving a piece of the heritage of an entire region.

Ethel Wright Mohamed's "memory pictures" are on display in the Mohamed family home, in a casual museum known simply as "Mama's Dream World." They offer an authentic taste of Delta life that no tour book or history book can provide.

Tybee Island lies off the Georgia coast, just slightly north of Savannah. It is the northernmost of Georgia's thirteen barrier islands. Tybee offers travelers a trip back in time. The pace of life here is slow, and the island has remained mostly unchanged since the 1950s, when most of its small hotels and cottages were built. The simple black and white tower of Tybee Light rises on the north coast of the island. Across the island, a museum at Old Fort Screven offers a glimpse into island history.

This rustic log building once served as both a school and a church meeting house for pioneers in Gadsden, Alabama. Today the building is part of a pioneer village recreation at Noccalula Falls Park. The park, which also features the Gilliland-Reese covered bridge and a pioneer museum, is located at the end of Lookout Mountain Parkway, a one-hundred-mile scenic drive that begins in Tennessee. The park is named after a waterfall that cascades ninety feet over a ledge on Lookout Mountain into a lush ravine.

*F*ROM LAKESHORES TO COOL NORTH WOODS,
the Great Lakes region awaits discovery
by the careful byway traveler. Each
of the states in this region
is touched by at least one of
our great inland seas, but each also
has its own distinctive allure.
The area offers the charm of the Amish,
boasts the peaceful roads
of its dairy country, and
proudly preserves the legends of
the pioneers. The region also
provides ample opportunity to
step off the beaten track and discover
the shores of the Great Lakes and beyond.

FROM LAKESHORES
TO COOL NORTH WOODS

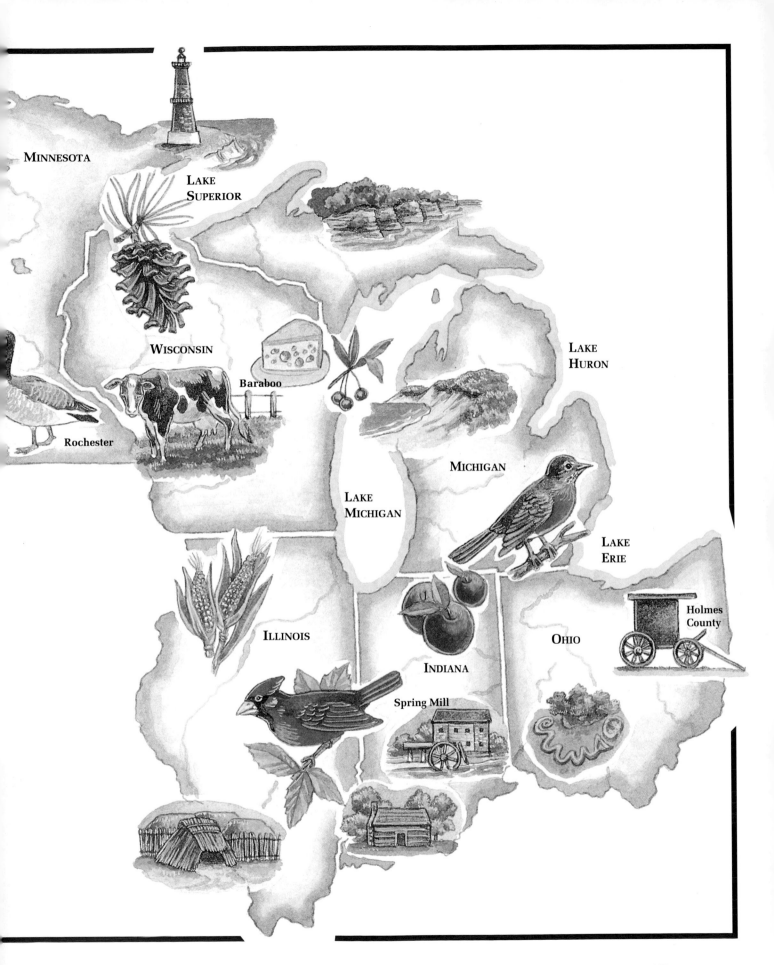

MINNESOTA

LAKE
SUPERIOR

WISCONSIN

Baraboo

Rochester

LAKE
HURON

MICHIGAN

LAKE
MICHIGAN

LAKE
ERIE

Holmes
County

ILLINOIS

OHIO

Spring Mill

INDIANA

Emerald Lake

Edna Jaques

If I could paint, I'd rest my easel there
Where all the wonders of the earth and sky
Would be reflected in this emerald lake,
Where clouds like white-winged ships would wander by,
Laden with jewels plucked from Nature's stores,
Showing the glory of the out of doors.

I'd paint a glistening sail of lapis blue
Upon the tarnished silver of the lake,
A great encircling mountain thatched with snow,
And saffron poppies where their gold would make
A flaming cluster in the green brocade
Of carpet moss and grassy cups of jade.

And in the foreground I would paint old rocks
With rusty seams and gray as weathered flint,
And sapphire walls with trailing rainbow lights
Playing upon the water's emerald tint,
A royal pageantry whose colors vie
With all the bright-hued splendors of the sky.

Split Rock Lighthouse is one highlight of the one-hundred-and-fifty-mile North Shore Drive along the rugged Minnesota coast of Lake Superior. The road winds from Duluth to Grand Portage, past some of the most spectacular scenery east of the Rockies. Split Rock Lighthouse sits on a rocky cliff one hundred and sixty-eight feet above the cold waters of Lake Superior. It has been a landmark for sailors and travelers on land for over sixty years.

The Great Lakes add a special dimension to life in each of the states touched by their waters. Michigan, perhaps most of all, is shaped by these great inland seas, with four of the five lakes meeting Michigan land. In fact, no point in the state is more than eighty-five miles from the lakeshore. Wisconsin, Minnesota, Illinois, Ohio, and even Indiana, with its small stretch of coastline on Lake Michigan, at some point see their flat stretches of farmland, rolling green hills, or dense woodlands give way to lakefront. Like coastal travelers, lakeshore travelers are drawn to the waterfront where they will find dramatic cliffs, abundant wildlife, rocky beaches, and the irresistible charm of coastline drives.

The more than eighty-four thousand square miles that make up Minnesota include more than five thousand square miles of water—including at least the ten thousand lakes the state's slogan boasts. One of these lakes, Rochester's Silver Lake, is the winter home to thousands of Canada geese, who cut their southward flight short. The birds are encouraged to stay by the abundant cornfields surrounding the lake, which provide food until the winter's snow cover descends, and by the local residents and bird lovers who come to visit the lake well stocked with feed for the geese.

Yoder's Amish Home

FOUR COUNTIES IN OHIO'S northeast corner—Holmes, Wayne, Tuscarawas, and Stark—are home to the largest concentration of Amish in the world. Descendants of sixteenth-century Swiss Protestant Anabaptists, the Amish believe in pacifism and self-reliance; and since they came to America over two hundred years ago, they have pursued agriculture as a way of life.

Yoder's Amish Home, between Trail and Walnut Creek in Holmes County, Ohio, is a hundred-acre working farm owned by Eli and Gloria Yoder. These two were raised in the Amish community but have decided to share their heritage with the many visitors who come to Ohio seeking a glimpse of the unique world of the Amish.

The Yoders offer guided tours of their home and farm. There are also buggy rides and a chance to buy the works of local Amish artisans, from patchwork quilts to hickory rockers.

Amish country holds an irresistible charm for Americans looking for a glimpse of life in a simpler form. For many, it is life the way it used to be when farms were self-sufficient, and telephone and electric wires didn't mar the country landscape.

Although a drive through Amish country can feel like a nostalgic journey through the past, these "old-fashioned" surroundings are very much the present for thousands of faithful Amish families. At the Yoder's home and in small towns and on country roads throughout northeastern Ohio, visitors respectful of the Amish people's right to a separate way of life are always welcome. The Amish are comfortable with their distinct, traditional way of life, and they are happy to share its simple secrets with thoughtful travelers.

Amish children play outside Yoder's Amish Home. With their charming straw hats and sunbonnets, Amish children are part of the picture-perfect scenes of country life that travelers find so endearing. But they are also part of a thriving American culture which values the family as the center of work, recreation, and education.

One of the Yoders' bedrooms features a beautiful hand-stitched quilt. Quilts, such as this one, draw travelers from across the country eager to make a piece of Amish stitchery their own family's heirloom.

Let Us
Go Back
Thomas Curtis Clark

Let us go back
To the simpler and better things;
Let us retrace our steps
From our greed-born bickerings
Back to the quietness
Of plain, good friendliness.

Most Amish still farm without the help of modern mechanical equipment, relying instead on horses and the hard work of family and community.

Let us go back
To the old roads of beauty's quest;
Let us again find joy
In the fields and the woods, possessed
By the thrill of the spring,
And of summer wandering.

Let us go back
To old-fashioned content, our wealth
Found in the garden nooks,
And beneath home roofs. Let the health
Of the trees and the grass
Be ours, as the seasons pass.

Spring Mill Village

IN PIONEER AMERICA, A GRIST mill often created a village. Such was the case in Spring Mill, Indiana, where a thriving pioneer village grew up around a handsome limestone mill built to grind corn for local farmers. Spring Mill's giant water wheel began turning in 1812. By 1814 it was a state of the art nineteenth-century grist mill: three stories of beautiful limestone with an eight-ton water wheel. Farmers from all over southern Indiana came to Spring Mill to turn their corn and wheat crops into meal. Crafts and tradespeople also came to Spring Mill to capture the business of the visiting farmers. Soon there were shops along a main street, and a boat yard on the banks of the nearby White River. From there, the people of Spring Mill could ship their goods all the way to New Orleans.

But the town that the mill built could not thrive forever. The mid-nineteenth century brought innovations that made the old water-driven mill obsolete; and railroad builders bypassed Spring Mill as they laid their tracks toward the West.

Later generations, proud of their local heritage and also entranced by the romance of the old grist mill, restored the village; it is now part of the Indiana state park system. Today, the grist mill still grinds grain the old-fashioned way. And travelers, looking for a bit of Americana on the backroads of southern Indiana, are welcome to stop and experience Spring Mill Village as it once was.

The old limestone grist mill at Spring Mill Village recalls a simpler time in America. The mill was built by some of the first pioneers to enter Indiana, most of whom came from Kentucky, Tennessee, and Virginia. They arrived in Indiana to find a great hardwood forest from the Appalachians to the Mississippi River; and with hard work and perseverance, they cleared land for their crops. Today, the traditions of the pioneers are maintained by many Hoosiers, as almost three quarters of Indiana's land is devoted to agriculture.

Dairy farming began in Wisconsin as part of a conservation movement. William Dempster Hoard, publisher of the newspaper Hoard's Dairyman, *saw that the once-rich soil of southern Wisconsin's farmland was being rapidly depleted by the intensive growing of wheat. He urged his fellow agriculturalists to turn to dairy farming to put less of a burden on the land. Hoard's message was heeded, and a new tradition was begun. Wisconsin quickly became the leading producer of milk, butter, and cheese in the United States; and beautiful vistas, like this one of a farmhouse nestled between lush green pastures near Baraboo, became Wisconsin's trademark. So committed did Wisconsin become to dairy farming that until 1960 the sale of the non-dairy product of margarine was forbidden.*

Abraham Lincoln's parents were part of a group of adventurous Kentucky farmers who crossed the Ohio River in the early nineteenth century searching for new land and a new life in the southern hills of Indiana. The future president was seven when the family made the move, old enough to help put up a rustic log cabin and begin the hard work of clearing farmland out of the dense forest. The cabin and surrounding farm have been rebuilt and are preserved as part of the Lincoln Boyhood National Monument, a tribute not only to a great president, but also to the pioneer spirit that helped create the state of Indiana.

ACROSS WINDSWEPT PLAINS AND FIELDS OF GRAIN,
the byways of the great plains are
straight and flat,
yet they hold treasures well worth
stopping to explore. In South Dakota,
a Native American festival
celebrates the arts of people who
have called the northern plains home
for centuries. In Iowa, a community
gathers to salute some of the most
charming covered bridges in all of
America. And across these wide open
spaces, the traveler is a welcome guest,
as residents eagerly share the
unique and wonderful experiences of
life on the plains.

ACROSS WINDSWEPT
PLAINS AND FIELDS OF GRAIN

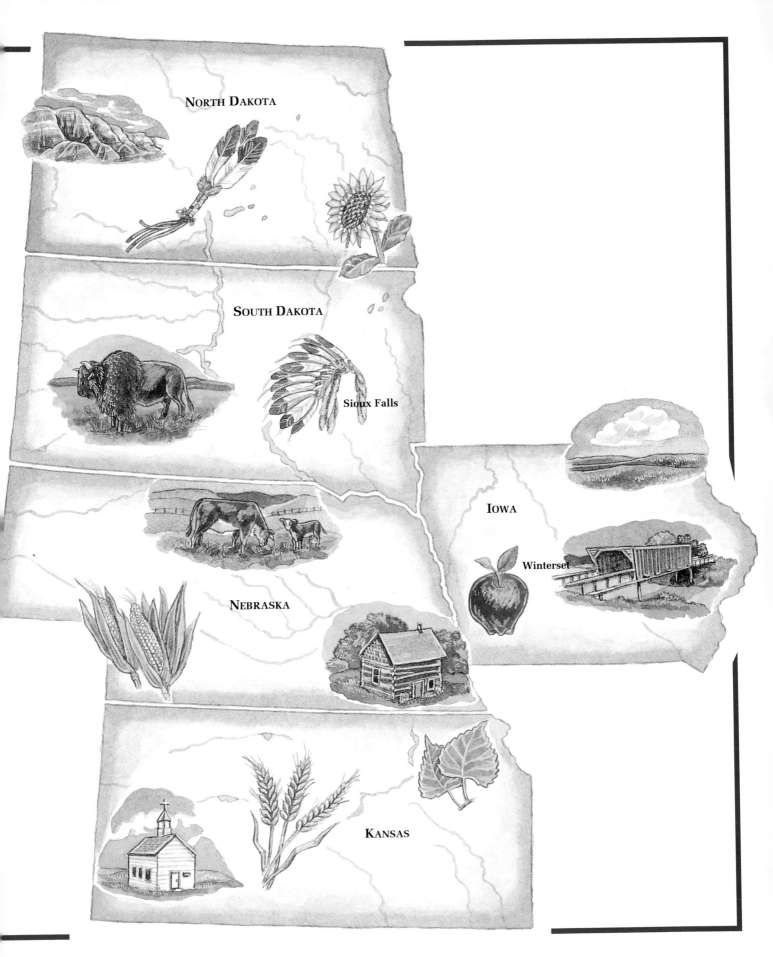

NORTH DAKOTA

SOUTH DAKOTA

Sioux Falls

IOWA

Winterset

NEBRASKA

KANSAS

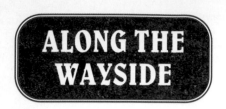

Plains Church
Grace Noll Crowell

Set like a jewel on this wind-swept plain,
Its clapboards rising upward from the sod,
The country church stands staunch through wind and rain,
And there they go for miles to worship God.
And they will find Him waiting for them there,
Far from the city's clamoring din and strife,
Among their own fields, swept with clean sweet air
Fragrant with the essences of life.

Within these walls life has its sacred part.
Here they bless the very young;
And many a heart has here been joined to heart;
And many a farewell hymn has been sung.
Here neighbor joins with neighbor; side by side
They praise our God beneath this endless sky.

The state of Kansas takes its name from the Sioux word Kansa, *which means "people of the south wind." The name remains apt. Despite the changes European settlers have made on the plains of Kansas, it is still the wind that defines life here, bringing hot southern air in the summer and brutal northern cold in the winter. With nothing but the wide open plains in its path, the Kansas wind whips and sweeps where it pleases, often making life on the plains a struggle against the weather.*

The Frontier

Michael D. Hull

A frontier waits to be breached
Out where new freedom shall be reached,
Along that distant timberline
Above the swift river, a sign
Of something clean, unknown, and new,
Untasted, like tomorrow's dew.
It calls to certain seeking men
Who come to find their answers when
Life's raucous pace, discordant roar,
Has dimmed their hope, has left them poor.
It is the sound of salmon leaping,
Of an old brown bear, awake from sleeping,
Of feathered wings upward rushing
From lofty pines, straining, hushing.
It is the pant of a running fox,
Cold water slapping on gleaming rocks.
It is the peace on a waiting hill
Where time, immense, is hourless, still.
There is man's widespread frontier—
Ancient yet new, far yet near,
Miles away from clocks and crowds,
Beneath the sun and wind and clouds.

South Dakota is still largely an undiscovered state, offering the byway traveler seemingly endless wide-open spaces. It is a place where one can see and feel what our early pioneers must have felt as they laid their eyes upon haunting vistas like those offered by the Badlands and the majestic, once-plentiful bison.

The Madison County Covered Bridge Festival

FOR A FEW DAYS EVERY October, the people of Madison County, Iowa, gather to celebrate the pride of their county: six one-hundred-and-ten-year-old wooden covered bridges. These six are what remain of a group of sixteen bridges, all covered in the same year in this section of south central Iowa. The bridges on display at festival time have been restored—some have even been moved—and all are

treasured remnants of a bygone era. Madison County hopes someday to bring the remaining ten bridges back to life, making the annual celebration an even grander event.

The festival features guided tours of the bridges, offering history and legend surrounding each. One might visit Holiwell Bridge, the longest in Madison County, whose planks are arranged in the shape of a giant bow; or Hogback Bridge, which still carries daily traffic in its original location. And it seems that each bridge has at least one bit of legend attached to it, like the bridge where a fugitive allegedly disappeared right before the eyes of his pursuers. Stories like this one, passed on by the locals from one generation to the next, only add to the charm and allure of these quaint old structures.

While the covered

Children try their hands at cider pressing.

bridges draw the crowds year after year, the festival is also a celebration of local culture as it existed in the 1880s when the bridges were built. Old-time craft demonstrations are the order of the day, with everything from candle dipping to sheep shearing to cider pressing carried out just as it was by Iowans of the late nineteenth century. Visitors can take advantage of booths set up by local artisans and purchase quality craft work, or they can try their hand at something their own great

Spinning fleece into yarn the old-fashioned way.

grandmother might have done, like making an authentic corn husk doll or spinning local fleece into yarn.

The Madison County Covered Bridge Festival is an event worth traveling for. The rainbow of license plate colors seen on Iowa country roads each October attests to the number of people who come to Madison County from far-off states for a celebration of a classic symbol of the American countryside and a revival of good old-fashioned American craftsmanship.

Northern Plains Tribal Arts

A tipi bag, decorated with beadwork, made by a member of the Rosebud Sioux tribe of South Dakota.

SEPTEMBER IN SIOUX FALLS, South Dakota, means only one thing: the annual celebration of the art of the Native American tribes of the northern plains. The annual Tribal Arts festival, at which art is both judged and sold, provides artists from the Sioux, Blackfeet, Chippewa, Cheyenne, Crow, and other plains tribes an outlet for their wonderful work. It also offers the general public a chance to make this distinctive American art a part of their own lives.

To many Americans, Native American art means only the turquoise jewelry and clay pots of the tribes of the Southwest. Those people attending the Tribal Arts show, however, find a mind-opening experience. The featured work is divided into two categories: the Tribal Arts, which include quillwork, beadwork, quilting, weaving, leatherwork, metalwork, and doll making; and the Fine Arts, which include sculpture, photography, and painting. Works in both categories are infused with the heritage and the symbolism of the Northern Plains tribes.

Art has always been especially important to the native

A parfleche box painted by a member of South Dakota's Oglala Sioux.

residents of the plains. As they had no written language, it was through art that their culture and traditions were preserved and passed on to succeeding generations. Through earth pigment paintings on animal hides, through exquisite, colorful quillwork decorations on clothing, through handcarved peace pipes, the plains people expressed their individuality and their tribal connections and left a record of their way of life without the benefit of written language. Although they suffered with the increasing westward movement of settlers, as their culture was threatened or destroyed, it is a tribute to the artists of the Northern Plains that their tradition has been maintained. In many cases they have incorporated the techniques from other cultures, but the art has remained strictly their own.

For the traveler wishing to experience modern Native American life beyond the stereotypes, the Tribal Arts show is a wonderful place to start, for one will not only find a preserved piece of history, but a gathering of thriving creative artists with a proud heritage.

THE CROSSROADS OF THE OLD WEST
once marked the far reaches
of the United States.
But this region's history goes back
to a time before there was a place
called America, back to the
Spanish, who came in the
fifteenth century, and to the
native peoples before them.
Today, the Old West proudly
celebrates each of the varied
elements of its heritage.
From the Taos pueblo, to an
old Spanish mission,
to a dulcimer jamboree in the Ozarks,
travelers to this region will find
history and tradition around every bend.

Taos

NEW MEXICO

CROSSROADS
OF THE OLD WEST

Lake of the Ozarks

MISSOURI

Mountain View

ARKANSAS

OKLAHOMA

TEXAS

Nacogdoches

Crockett

San Antonio

Trails of Past and Now

Anton J. Stoffle

Over the countryside I roam,
With the west wind at my brow,
Through the meadows, beyond the streams,
On the trails of past and now.

I trod o'er the footsteps made before—
In a distant age and day—
By the lonely gait of a wayfarer,
Who was either sad or gay.

Somehow I cannot help but feel
That this someone felt as I,
When roaming o'er the countryside
In the good old by-and-by.

Perhaps with a song upon his lips,
Though funny as it seems,
The vagabond who traveled here
May have shared my special dreams.

But nevertheless I wander
Where the sunlight kisses the sod,
Where solitude brings pleasure,
And a man can speak with God.

Over the countryside I roam,
With the west wind at my brow,
Through the meadows, beyond the streams,
On the trails of past and now.

Cotton was responsible for the livelihood of many along the Mississippi River in Arkansas in the years before the Civil War, just as it was throughout the South. But the rustic old Cross Creek rice mill attests to a different part of Arkansas' agricultural past. The flat, fertile lands west of the great Mississippi proved perfect for growing rice; and as the years passed, cotton gave way to rice as Arkansas' leading crop. Today, the state provides more rice than any other in the nation, although mills like this one—made obsolete by modern technology—are now valued for nostalgic, rather than practical, purposes.

The Grist Mill

Shirley Ruth Boyd

In the dark and dusty mill I stand;
I can hear it crack and groan.
I can hear a splashing noise outside;
I can hear the mill wheel moan.
I stand and dream of bygone days
When in this very place
The miller stood and plied his trade
With flour upon his face
Near the platform where the wagons came
To bring their grain and corn,
And this one where they got their flour
From the miller that next morn.
I think I hear the splashing
Of the mill wheel turning round.
Is it overshot or undershot?
I listen as it's ground.
A shaft of sunlight filters through
A broken window pane,
And golden, in the sunbeams,
Little dust motes dance again.
The little stream keeps flowing on
Beside the old grist mill,
Although the wheel that one day turned
Sits silent, mournful, still.

This old grist mill sits on the banks of the Jacks Forks River in the Ozark Mountains of southeastern Missouri. Over a hundred miles of the Jacks Forks and nearby Current rivers are designated as the Ozark National Scenic Riverways. Along their banks are woodland cabins, historic small towns, hot springs, caves, and spectacular bluffs. The best way to travel the area is by boat on an old-fashioned Missouri float trip.

Ozark Dulcimer Jamboree

EACH SPRING FOR THE PAST fifteen years, the country's dulcimer players and dulcimer enthusiasts have gathered in Mountain View, Arkansas, for the annual Ozark Folk Center Dulcimer Jamboree. The dulcimer is an ancient instrument that has been a part of the culture of the Ozarks since the first settlers came to these mountains years ago. The jamboree features workshops, lessons, performances, and competitions in which the top players vie

for the honor of being named the year's best on the Mountain Dulcimer, on the Hammered Dulcimer, and in the Ensemble.

The dulcimers at the jamboree are the finest examples of a traditional craft. The best dulcimers are made by hand out of carefully chosen, finely grained walnut and spruce. After the wood is dried to the precise moisture content of six or seven percent, each piece is cut and sanded with great care. There is no absolute standard for the shape of the dulcimer; true to its heritage as a mountain craft, each instrument bears the mark of its particular artisan: some designs pass from parent to child while others are particular to a town or a county. Walnut is used to make a dulcimer in rich, warm browns; spruce gives a contrasting top piece of yellow. Once the pieces are assembled, hours of fine hand-sanding and precise tuning take place before the finished product is ready for the strumming of such old-time favorites as "Boil Them Cabbage Down" or the more detailed picking of a classic tune like "Jesu, Joy of Man's Desiring."

At Mountain View's Dulcimer Shoppe, they say that anyone who can count to ten can learn to play the dulcimer. But easy as it may be to learn the technical skills, it takes a love and appreciation for the unique culture of the Ozarks to play good old-fashioned "mountain music."

At the Ozark Folk Center State Park, the dulcimer jamboree is just one of many events that celebrate the local Ozark Mountain culture. There are folk dances, gospel concerts, autoharp workshops, herb festivals, and more; each event keeps alive a part of Ozark tradition. And there are always local artisans at the Center practicing their crafts, offering demonstrations, and displaying goods for sale. Workshops teach visitors how to weave a basket or how to make a corn shuck doll, while performers like these keep everyone dancing with the old mountain music.

The Need of Being Versed in Country Things

Robert Frost

The house had gone to bring again
To the midnight sky a sunset glow.
Now the chimney was all of the house that stood,
Like a pistil after the petals go.

The barn opposed across the way,
That would have joined the house in flame
Had it been the will of the wind, was left
To bear forsaken the place's name.

No more it opened with all one end
For teams that came by the stony road
To drum on the floor with scurrying hoofs
And brush the mow with the summer load.

The birds that came to it through the air
At broken windows flew out and in,
Their murmur more like the sigh we sigh
From too much dwelling on what has been.

Yet for them the lilac renewed its leaf,
And the aged elm, though touched with fire;
And the dry pump flung up an awkward arm;
And the fence post carried a strand of wire.

For them there was really nothing sad.
But though they rejoiced in the nest they kept,
One had to be versed in country things
Not to believe the phoebes wept.

The Ozark Mountain region stretches from northwestern Arkansas west into Oklahoma and north toward central Missouri. It is a land of steep hills, deep hollows, thousands of limestone caves, and more than ten thousand natural springs. It is also a land rich in pioneer heritage. Old abandoned farms like this one, tucked into the woods near Missouri's Lake of the Ozarks, remind modern travelers of the people who came before: brave pioneers who made their homes in isolated villages and who gave this area its unique and colorful history.

CROSSROADS HERITAGE

El Camino Real

RUNNING FROM THE RIO Grande River in southwestern Texas northeastward to the Louisiana border near Nacogdoches is what Texans proudly call *El Camino Real*, a Spanish phrase for "the royal road." This is the oldest trans-Texas route, which is really a series of roads along which one can discover the heritage of the people, common folks and great leaders alike, who made the great state of Texas.

El Camino Real is actually four roads that combine to cross the state: Camino de los Tejas, Lower Presidio Road, Upper Presidio Road, and Camino Arriba. The earliest section of the road officially dates to 1691; but the route existed even earlier in old Comanche and Apache trails, natural stream crossings, and explorers' routes.

The heritage of El Camino Real is distinctly Spanish and dates from the days when much of Texas was owned by Mexico. A drive down this historic route might lead to a beautiful San Antonio mission, perhaps the legendary Alamo, or Nuestra Senora de la Purisima Concepcion.

These elegant stone missions, left behind by the Spanish, add character and charm to the Texas landscape along El Camino Real. One will also discover evidence of the state's more ancient history along the route. Remains of ancient homes and villages and intriguing arrangements of Native American mounds lie along the roadside and across the surrounding landscape.

Of course, Texas history also abounds along El Camino Real. The route was vital in the early history of the Republic of Texas and allowed settlers to enter the state and made communication across its great expanses possible. Travelers can explore towns like Crockett, which celebrates the legendary American frontiersman Davy Crockett, and Nacogdoches, which is a repository of Texas revolutionary history.

El Camino Real takes a traveler across the great expanse of central Texas, into the heart of the rich and varied cultural heritage of a proud and storied state.

The land that is now the state of Texas had a rich history—long before it became a part of the United States of America—as part of the vast Spanish empire that spread northward from Mexico. In Texas revolutionary days, residents fought hard to prove themselves independent, but today the legacy of the Spanish, including the San Antonio missions, the architecture, the food, and the language, is a treasured part of what sets Texas apart from every other state in the Union.

The Mission Church

Evelyn S. Dickey

Quiet by the old highway
A church of stone serenely stands,
Spires pointing ever skyward,
Foundation resting in His hands.

Throaty bells still softly chime
From their lofty tower in age-old brass,
Calling all the faithful homeward,
Beckoning to those who pass.

English ivy, moist roots anchored
In the life-sustaining ground,
Curls its tendrils toward the sunbeams,
Twines the weathered church around.

Like the verdant ivy, climbing
Upward in our heaven-search,
Must we rise with faith our foothold
In the little gray stone church.

Mission Nuestra Senora de la Purisima Concepcion, in San Antonio, is the oldest unrestored stone church in the United States. Twenty years in construction, the mission was completed in 1755 by Franciscan friars. The impressive church has twin towers and a cupola. Experts have compared the acoustics of this beautiful old stone church to Utah's famed Mormon Tabernacle.

The Taos Pueblo, in north central New Mexico, has been home to the Taos Indians for almost eight centuries. The massive adobe structure rests on a wide plateau on the banks of the Rio Pueblo de Taos. In the distance rises New Mexico's tallest peak, Mount Wheeler. The heritage of the Taos and other Pueblo tribes—many still thriving in the region—is evident in the architecture, the language, and the art of New Mexico.

Long before the English began to settle America's East Coast, Spanish ranchers made their way north from Mexico by following the Rio Grande and settled in what is now central New Mexico. Missions and ranches sprang up along the Rio Grande in the late 1500s; and by 1610, still ten years before the Pilgrims landed at Plymouth, the Spanish ranchers founded the town of Santa Fe. American settlers from the East did not begin to arrive until almost two hundred years later when the Santa Fe Trail, which traced a route into New Mexico from Missouri, made travel into the region possible from the East. By the second half of the nineteenth century, New Mexico was United States' territory; but the culture of the Spanish ranchers, which had been a part of the region for more than three hundred years, remains a special part of life in New Mexico.

*THROUGH RUGGED MOUNTAIN PASSES,
where sharp-edged peaks rise against
crystal clear skies and offer views
more breathtaking than anywhere else
in America, the byways of the West
are spectacular. Yet there is more to
this region than its scenery.
In Arizona one can discover the ancient
history of the Navajo, a people who have
shaped so much of the culture of the
Southwest. Further north, one can join in
a cowboy festival celebrating the rugged
men and women who first conquered the
Rocky Mountains. And throughout the region,
travelers who come expecting only
spectacular scenery will find fascinating
stories to go along with their snapshots.*

THROUGH RUGGED
MOUNTAIN PASSES

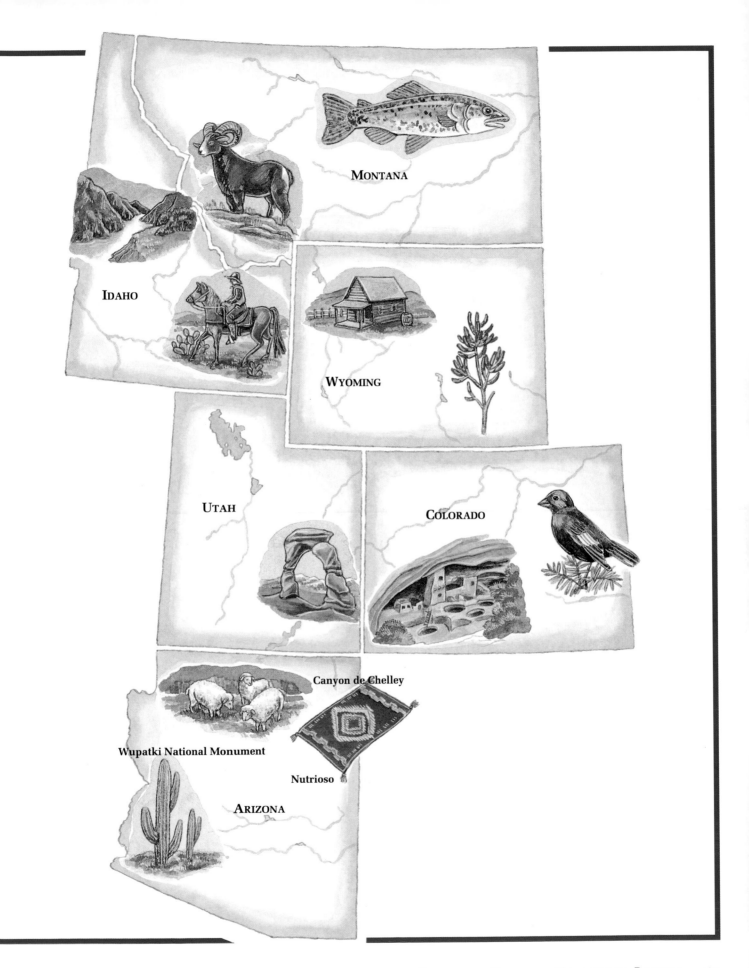

MONTANA

IDAHO

WYOMING

UTAH

COLORADO

Canyon de Chelley

Wupatki National Monument

Nutrioso

ARIZONA

Cabin

Joy Belle Burgess

This cabin is here because someone dared
To face the new frontier,
With oxen and plow and bucksaw blade,
Through the seasons, year after year.

The ancient floor is treaded and worn
With remembrances that last,
Of old caulked boots and lumberjacks
And whining blades from the past.

The valiant sill crumbles with age,
And the cabin stands alone;
Tall fir trees spread their sheltering boughs
And claim it as their own.

The boarded walls are covered with moss
Like the sagging roof and beams,
And still, its spell won't let me go
But holds me here to dream.

Wyoming is famous for its great natural wonders: the geysers of Yellowstone, the rugged peaks of the Rockies, the abundant wildlife in its natural parks. But the careful traveler looks for the backroads, where sights like this lonely mountain barn speak of the real Wyoming: a land settled and still populated by rugged individuals with great respect for the land. In the early days, settlers gave their new homes romantic names like Bighorn and Yellowstone to try and lure friends and neighbors from the East. (They weren't hungry for neighbors, just for the population to meet requirements for statehood.) Today, with statehood secured, the people of Wyoming are pleased to report that their state holds the honor of being the nation's least populated.

Desert Roads

Lorraine Ussher Babbitt

With sleek, sophisticated curves,
The highway flaunts its purposed path
Along the mountain's base;
Then suddenly, with rocket-like
Economy of line,
It plunges out across
The desert miles
Devouring distance with swift certainty,
To disappear, a silver dot
Upon the far horizon rim.

But in its wake,
The desert lies unmoved
And smiling;
On its aged face
A thousand tiny roads crisscross.
From rabbit hole
To hidden spring,
From wind-carved butte
To briefly reeded lakes of sand,
From green mesquite
Through Joshuas, weird
Suppliant forms, they go,
These winsome desert roads
That flash and wind,
That run and vanish
In a rocky wash—
Smile lines upon the desert's face.

Most people picture Arizona as a state dominated by desert—a hot, dry land covered by canyons and saguaro cacti. In truth, desert covers only one percent of the over one hundred thousand square miles that make up Arizona. The Sonora Desert, in the southwestern corner, is the state's only true desert. The remainder is mostly scrub desert which supports a wide variety of plant and animal life. This windmill is in Nutrioso, Arizona.

High Country Cowboy Festival

FOR THREE DAYS EACH July, the people of Idaho gather at the base of the Grand Teton Mountains, near the Wyoming border, to celebrate the culture of the West. This annual event, called the High Country Cowboy Festival, includes everything from cowboy poets to western swing dancing to tales from the days of the western frontier.

The Teton Valley of Idaho is, and has been for more than one hundred years, cattle country. On wide rolling plains beneath the thirteen-thousand-foot peaks of the Tetons, backroads lead to weathered old ranchers' cabins and endless herds of white-faced cattle grazing contentedly. Life for Teton ranchers has never been easy: winters are cold and harsh, summers can bring unyielding heat, and the very mountains that make this region one of the most spectacular in all of America have always meant a certain amount of isolation. Even today eastern Idaho, like many of the mountainous regions in our West, is a sparsely populated land, drawing many visitors but few permanent residents.

The annual Idaho High Country Cowboy Festival pays tribute to all who have called eastern Idaho home, from the early settlers who began the ranching tradition to those residents who continue it today.

Horses were an indispensable part of life on the western frontier. They pulled the wagons that carried settlers from the East, they helped farmers clear and cultivate the land, and they served as constant companions and partners for the cowboys who made the enormous cattle ranches possible. Seen here grazing beneath the spectacular Sawtooth Mountains in Stanley, Idaho, horses are a symbol of the heritage and modern culture of the rugged American West.

Monument Valley Navajo Tribal Park

IN THE FIFTEENTH CENTURY, the Navajo people migrated south from their ancestral home in what is now Canada to the Colorado Plateau in what would one day become northeastern Arizona. There they found a flat, barren landscape and dry, scorching heat. But they also found a spectacular canyon—called Canyon de Chelley—which held the ruins of remarkable cliff dwellings carved out of the red sandstone. The dwellings had been built by the Anasazi people almost two hundred years earlier. These homes were abandoned soon thereafter when the diminished water supply made their agricultural way of life impossible in the canyon.

The Navajo ended their migration inside Canyon de Chelley and began a way of life that worked with what little the harsh desert landscape provided, a way of life they maintain to this day.

Five hundred years later, much of the culture of the southwest is the culture of the Navajo and other native tribes that have made a home amidst the deserts and canyons of the Colorado Plateau. Travelers who explore the dry, dusty backroads can discover such wondrous sights as Betatakin, which means "ledge house" in Navajo. This multi-leveled cliff dwelling is a fine example of Anasazi architecture. It is not a separate structure but a part of the natural landscape, in perfect harmony with its surroundings. Perhaps it is this fact that has allowed Betatakin to last through the centuries. A strenuous three-mile hike leads to the rose-colored cliff dwelling itself, while a less taxing half-mile walk opens on an overlook of Betatakin. From a distance this cliff dwelling looks almost impossibly nestled into the sheer face of sandstone.

Inside Canyon de Chelley, winding scenic drives present breathtaking views of steep canyon walls and eight-hundred-foot spires. Navajo still live in the canyon much as they have for more than five hundred years. Respectful visitors are welcome to witness the magnificent ruins and the extraordinary lifestyle of the people who make their homes on these arid high plains.

Unlike the Anasazi people who lived in Canyon de Chelley in northeastern Arizona before them, the Navajo did not try to support themselves by growing crops on the arid desert land. They relied, instead, upon sheep herding as their main means of survival, supplemented by growing corn and squash where possible on the flat canyon floor. Their ability to make the most of their natural surroundings has allowed the Navajo to remain in this inhospitable environment for almost five hundred years.

Weaving is a traditional Navajo craft. Sheep herding has been a way of life for Navajo men since they first arrived in the Southwest hundreds of years ago; and for just as long, it has been the task of Navajo women to turn the raw wool into brightly colored blankets and garments. The process involves cleaning, carding, spinning, dyeing, and, finally, weaving on handcrafted looms. The Navajo blanket has become an instantly recognizable symbol of the Southwest, and its traditional patterns are copied in furniture, art, and clothing.

Fine Small Blanket

Maude Rubin

She sits by the loom through the sun-long day
Of this ageless desert land,
Weaving a blanket as bright as play,
As soft as a baby's hand.

She has carded and spun the lamb-soft wool
Till it shines like ripened wheat;
She has dipped it in colors of the desert dawn
To warm a small one's feet.

Her design is the rainbow, the moon and the sun;
She weaves till the shadows are thinned,
But she longs for the day when the blanket is done
And lullabies ride on the wind.

Like most of the Southwest, Arizona has its share of deserted old towns, or remnants
of towns, which tell the story of mining days, when the lure of gold, silver, copper, and
turquoise brought prospectors and prosperity to isolated desert locations. The remains
of these towns, which declined as quickly as they arose once the ore ran out, hold an
eerie fascination for travelers today. Often standing alone amid miles of desert landscape, the shells of these once booming towns offer a glimpse into history and a testa-
ment to the endurance of this wonderful, harsh land.

Although the states of the Southwest were some of the last to join the union, they have the most ancient history of all America, having been home to native people for centuries. Wupatki National Monument is a tribute to one of the lesser known peoples of Arizona's past, the Sinaguas, who took advantage of a volcanic eruption to build a prosperous settlement near Sunset Crater. Volcanic ash from a 1064 eruption created a fertile layer of soil, of which the Sinaguan people were quick to make use. They built a settlement of pueblo dwellings, including a remarkable one-hundred-room, four-story building. The Singuan people left the area after less then two hundred years—perhaps because the rich soil had been depleted—but their sandstone structures remain.

FRONTIER TRACKS TO THE PACIFIC,
first laid down by settlers along the
Oregon Trail, still lead byway travelers
to the West Coast. In Washington, the
great wheat farms of the east give way to
dramatic coastal scenes; in Nevada,
ghost towns dot the landscape, telling
the story of the Wild West; and in
Hawaii, the most commonplace vistas
are made spectacular by the tropical
backdrops. Central to the region is the
great expanse of the Pacific, which shapes
the culture of the American West.

FRONTIER TRACKS
TO THE PACIFIC

ALASKA

WASHINGTON

Walla Walla

OREGON

Charleston

HAWAII

CALIFORNIA

Virginia City

NEVADA

Ely

Pioche

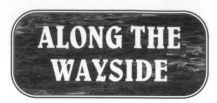

To The Depths

Edna Greene Hines

As far as the eye can see, I looked.
These were the things I saw:
Sky and sea and sunlit waves
All bound by Creation's law.

As far as the ear can hear, I heard
The winds and the waves of the sea,
With the ebb and flow of endless tides
And the birds in a willow tree.

As deep in my heart as I can feel,
I loved the sounds I heard;
For I was one with wind and wave
And the beauty of singing bird.

"I beheld the grandest and most pleasing prospects which my eyes ever surveyed . . . a boundless ocean . . . raging with immense waves and breaking with great force from the rocks." So remarked explorer William Clark in 1805 when he first laid eyes upon Oregon's coast. Clark, like the pioneers who would follow him in the rush of "Oregon fever," had braved a treacherous journey across the Snake River Gorge and the Cascade Mountains to reach the fertile Willamette Valley and the fantastic rocky Pacific Coast. Today, travel to Oregon's coast is far less difficult, but the rewards are just as sweet. Pictured here is a stretch of Shore's Acres State Park near Charleston on Oregon's southern coast.

Neither Out Far Nor In Deep

Robert Frost

The people along the sand
All turn and look one way.
They turn their back on the land.
They look at the sea all day.

As long as it takes to pass
A ship keeps raising its hull;
The wetter ground like glass
Reflects a standing gull.

The land may vary more;
But wherever the truth may be—
The water comes ashore,
And the people look at the sea.

They cannot look out far.
They cannot look in deep.
But when was that ever a bar
To any watch they keep?

Hawaii is truly an American national treasure, an island paradise cut off by more than two thousand miles of the Pacific that we can proudly call our own. Travelers are lured to Hawaii by the promise of white sandy beaches and warm sea breezes, but they will find other sights, both familiar and exotic. The Kilauea Lighthouse perches atop a lone cliff on the island of Kauai's north shore. It is not unlike the lighthouses seen on the coasts of New England or California, except for the lush green land that serves as its backdrop, part of a state park full of tropical vegetation and native seabirds. It is on the rugged coast of Kauai that English captain James Cook first landed in 1778 and revealed these wonderful volcanic islands to the Western world.

Nevada's Ghost Towns

TRAVELERS COME TO ELY, IN west central Nevada, to ride "The Ghost Train of Old Ely." This wonderfully preserved section of the historic Nevada Northern Railway was one of the last great mining railways built in America. After its completion in 1906, the Nevada Northern carried passengers until 1938 and freight until 1983. Today, the train carries passengers once more. An old No. 40 Baldwin ten-wheeler pulls an authentic 1890 Pullman coach full of travelers intent upon exploring the old town of Ely, one of Nevada's historic ghost towns.

Ghost towns are the abandoned remains of the mining towns that sprang up during the nineteenth century throughout Nevada. Some of the towns have been restored to become major tourist attractions; others lie well off the beaten track, with only the frames of a few buildings to testify to the bustling downtown that used to be. Each tells the story of a different era, when the promise of gold, silver, copper, and turquoise drew eager prospectors to Nevada from the East. With the rush of settlers came the towns, which thrived on the constant influx of people and money. Buildings rose seemingly overnight, and the once barren desert was suddenly dotted with boomtowns.

When the ore ran out, those who had come to Nevada with dreams of great wealth moved on; and the towns they had built were left to the heat and the sands of the desert. Many settlements disappeared entirely, fading from history as they faded from sight. Others hung on and remain today to tempt travelers with their eerie silence and to reveal to the observant visitor stories of an exciting era in the history of the West.

For fifty years, Virginia City was the most important of Nevada's mining boomtowns, producing over four hundred million dollars worth of silver and gold. The city was born in 1859 when two miners discovered gold at Six-Mile Canyon in western Nevada. They soon learned that gold wasn't the only thing in their new claim: a sticky blue mud that annoyingly coated their picks and shovels as they worked turned out to be pure silver ore, assayed at the 1859 price of two thousand dollars a ton. The two miners became millionaires; and their camp became Virginia City, with a six-story hotel, an opera house, and countless mansions. A devastating fire in 1875 destroyed almost two thousand of Virginia City's buildings; but as the money continued to pour in, most were rebuilt in only a year. It wasn't until the early twentieth century that the ore ran out and Virginia City began to be transformed from a boomtown into a ghost town. Today it can still claim itself a leader among mining towns: this time as one of the best preserved. Virginia City in the late twentieth century offers the most complete view into the life of a mining boom town, with its streets and buildings frozen in the time when it was known all over the world as the "richest place on earth."

Pioche was once known as the "toughest town in Nevada." This was truly the "Wild West," with miners frequently taking the law into their own hands. Located in southeastern Nevada, almost two hundred miles northeast of Las Vegas, Pioche experienced its boom in the late nineteenth century. Evidence of the abundance of money in the town is the Lincoln County Court House which cost almost one million dollars to build, a sum unheard of in those days. Pictured here are the remains of the Mountain View Hotel.

More than two thousand prospectors rushed to Midas, Nevada, in 1908 after rumors spread that a new vein of gold had been struck. Not much remains of Midas today because not much ever existed. The rumors of gold proved to be exaggerated. The ore was there, but not only was there not enough to support the rush of prospectors, but it lacked the quality of ore readily found elsewhere. So the prospectors packed up and moved on, leaving behind only a small group of cabins and rustic buildings: the ghost of a town that never really was.

The Great Northwest
George McDonald

From where the Cascade's mantled peaks
In silent beauty stand,
One travels east and comes upon
A vast midsummer wonderland.
Here on the broad and fertile plains
Roll wave on wave of golden grains;
And on the hills where cattle graze
Cloud shadows play on summer days;
And, in between, great rivers run,
In deep ravines, as chariots run,
To see which one the first shall be
To reach the waiting mother sea;
And here and there tall poplars rise
To live with hawks and clouds and skies
And mark the place where dwellings stand
As homes of folks who farm the land.

Here under open skies and wide
Live men and women of zeal and pride
And yet, withal, a comradery,
A pioneer simplicity
That knows no bounds, nor vague unrest:
This is our home, this great Northwest.

Much of eastern Washington looks just like this farm near Walla Walla: ribbons of road winding through endless fields of wheat that stretch to the horizon. These fertile farmlands are a far cry from the semi-arid plains that confronted the first settlers to come to this region over one hundred years ago. The Columbia Plateau, which stretches from Walla Walla in the south up beyond Spokane, is deprived of the rain that blesses western Washington. Eastern farmers owe their success to irrigation, the crowning achievement of which is the Grand Coulee Dam on the Columbia River.

Red Barns in Green Pastures

Doris K. Sutcliffe

Red gables cover bright timothy bales
And stand in the weather like fishermen's sails
Blending with seasons, as friend bows to friend,
"We are what we are, so let's not pretend."

Barns painted red bring green pastures to life;
The two are connected, like husband and wife.
Red barns are badges of faith in the land,
Brave and undaunted. I think they are grand!

So let's paint them red for the courage they hold,
Permanent glory on landscapes, so bold
And always unfading, a chanticleer hue.
In the quick summer morning they glisten with dew.

Real as the boulders and right as the rain,
Red barns are banners, all four-square and plain.
Here in the country they accent the charms
Of culture and crops and old family farms.

It is a miracle that settlers stopped on the dry, hostile lands of Washington's Columbia Plateau. Perhaps they decided they had come too far to turn back and were too weary of the road to attempt to cross the rugged Cascades to the more fertile land along the Pacific coast. Whatever the case, they decided to try their luck at farming; and with innovative irrigation, perseverance, and a strong sense of community, they succeeded. Today the Columbia Plateau boasts the richest wheat-growing land in the United States, as well as internationally recognized apple orchards and vineyards. It is also known for its rich pioneer heritage as farmers hold proudly to the ideals of their forefathers.

Separated by miles of ocean and a climate considered exotic on the mainland, Hawaii is, nonetheless, part of America, and its byways offer similar, if distinct, experiences. Island backroads lead to quiet country churches, just as on the mainland; only the backdrop of palm trees instead of maples sets them apart.

The influence of the Spanish can be seen and felt up and down the California coast—from the towns that have made their Spanish names a part of the American language to the elegant old churches left behind by the Spanish missionaries. Pictured here is Mission San Diego De Alcola.

INDEX

PHOTO CREDITS

6-7, Johnson's Photography; **8**, Dick Dietrich Photos; **11**, Dianne Dietrich Leis; **13**, Johnson's Photography; **14-15**, Johnson's Photography; **16**, Dianne Dietrich Leis; **17**, Johnson's Photography; **20**, Johnson's Photography; **22-23**, Johnson's Photography; **25**, Johnson's Photography; **27**, Hancock Shaker Village; **28-29**, Johnson's Photography; **30**, Johnson's Photography; **31**, Dianne Dietrich Leis; **35**, Johnson's Photography; **36**, Johnson's Photography; **38-39**, Pennsylvania Dutch Convention and Visitors Bureau; **40-41**, Johnson's Photography; **43**, Johnson's Photography; **47**, Dick Dietrich Photos; **48-49**, Dick Dietrich Photos; **52-55**, Blue Ridge Institute, Ferrum College, Ferrum, Virginia; **57**, Adam Jones; **60-61**, Johnson's Photography; **62-63**, Adam Jones; **64-65**, Adam Jones; **67**, Adam Jones; **68**, Johnson's Photography; **69**, Johnson's Photography; **70**, Johnson's Photography; **71**, Johnson's Photography; **72**, Adam Jones; **73**, Johnson's Photography; **77**, Adam Jones; **78**, Johnson's Photography; **80-81**, Dick Dietrich Photos; **83**, Blairsville, Georgia, Jaycees; **84-85**, Stitchery pictures by Ethel Wright Mohamed, courtesy of Mama's Dream World; **86**, Johnson's Photography; **87**, Johnson's Photography; **90-91**, Dick Dietrich Photos; **92-93**, Adam Jones; **94-97**, Yoder's Amish Home; **98-99**, Spring Mill State Park; **100**, Dick Dietrich Photos; **101**, Johnson's Photography; **106**, Dick Dietrich Photos; **107-108**, Dick Dietrich Photos; **108-111**, Madison County, Iowa, Covered Bridge Festival; **112-113**, Tribal Arts, '93, Sioux City, South Dakota; **117**, Dick Dietrich Photos; **119**, Dick Dietrich Photos; **120-121**, Ozark Folk Center State Park; **122-123**, Dick Dietrich Photos; **125**, Dick Dietrich Photos; **127**, Dick Dietrich Photos; **128**, Dick Dietrich Photos; **129**, Dick Dietrich Photos; **132**, Dick Dietrich Photos; **134**, Dick Dietrich Photos; **136-137**, Dick Dietrich Photos; **139**, Dick Dietrich Photos; **140**, Dick Dietrich Photos; **143**, Adam Jones; **146**, Dick Dietrich Photos; **148**, Dick Dietrich Photos; **150-153**, Nevada Commission on Tourism; **155**, Dick Dietrich Photos; **156-157**, Dick Dietrich Photos; **158**, Dick Dietrich Photos; **159**, Dick Dietrich Photos.

ACKNOWLEDGMENTS

SUMMER by Hal Borland reprinted by permission of Frances Collin, Literary Agent. Copyright © 1957 by Hal Borland. Copyright renewed © 1985 by Barbara Dodge Borland; EVENING IN A SUGAR ORCHARD and OCTOBER from *THE POETRY OF ROBERT FROST* edited by Edward Connery Lathem. Copyright 1923, 1930, © 1969 by Henry Holt and Company, Inc. Copyright © 1962 by Robert Frost. Reprinted by permission of Henry Holt and Company, Inc.; THE NEED OF BEING VERSED IN COUNTRY THINGS and NEITHER OUT FAR NOR IN DEEP from *THE POETRY OF ROBERT FROST* edited by Edward Connery Lathem. Copyright 1936, 1951 by Robert Frost. Copyright © 1964 by Lesley Ballantine Frost. Copyright 1923, © 1969 by Henry Holt and Co., Inc. Reprinted by permission of Henry Holt and Co., Inc.; EMERALD LAKE from *BESIDE STILL WATERS* by Edna Jaques, published in Canada by Thomas Allen & Son Limited; STABILITY from *THE GOLDEN ROAD* by Edna Jaques, published in Canada by Thomas Allen & Son Limited. Our sincere thanks to the following authors whom we were unable to contact: Lorraine Ussher Babbitt for DESERT ROADS; Thomas Curtis Clark for LET US GO BACK; Grace Noll Crowell for PLAINS CHURCH; Evelyn S. Dickey for THE MISSION CHURCH; Erma Stull Grove for THE COVERED BRIDGE; Michael D. Hull for THE FRONTIER; Lydia O. Jackson for THE OLD SPINNING WHEEL; George McDonald for THE GREAT NORTHWEST; and Maude Rubin for FINE SMALL BLANKET.

B 2
C 3
D 4
E 5
F 6
G 7
H 8
I 9
J 0